DIXON

V.

PROVIDENTIAL LIFE INSURANCE COMPANY

Seventh Edition

DIXON

V.

PROVIDENTIAL LIFE INSURANCE COMPANY

Seventh Edition

Adapted by

Edward R. Stein
Attorney at Law
Ann Arbor, Michigan

and

Frank D. Rothschild
Attorney at Law
Hanalei, Kauai, Hawaii

Original Case File by James H. Seckinger
Professor of Law
University of Notre Dame

NATIONAL INSTITUTE FOR TRIAL ADVOCACY

Address inquiries to:

Reprint Permission
National Institute for Trial Advocacy
1685 38th Street, Suite 200
Boulder, CO 80301-2735
Phone: (800) 225-6482
Fax: (720) 890-7069
Email: permissions@nita.org

ISBN 978-1-60156-7-994
eISBN 978-1-60156-8-007
FBA 1799

Printed in the United States of America

 Wolters Kluwer

Official co-publisher of NITA.
WKLegaledu.com/NITA

CONTENTS

INTRODUCTION

This is a contract action on a life insurance policy brought in the Nita State Court by Mary Dixon against the Providential Life Insurance Company. Mrs. Dixon is the beneficiary of a life insurance policy issued by the company insuring her husband, John Dixon. Mrs. Dixon found her husband dead with his hunting shotgun lying beside him. The cause of death was shotgun wounds to the head.

Mrs. Dixon claims that her husband's death was an accident, and she brings suit for the proceeds of a $1,000,000 life insurance policy with a double indemnity provision for accidental death. The Providential Life Insurance Company asserts that Mr. Dixon's death was a suicide, thus limiting its liability under the terms of the policy to the premiums paid.

Assume that there are no statutory presumptions relating to cause of death or suicide/accident in Nita. There is, however, a common-law presumption of a natural love of life and against a sane person taking his or her own life. Under the case law in Nita, suicide has been defined as the intentional, knowing, and conscious taking of one's own life.

With the exception of Mary Dixon, Sarah Lawton, and Anna Martin, all witnesses are written to be gender and race neutral. They may be played by a person of any gender or ethnic background.

All years in these materials are stated in the following form:

- YR-0 represents the actual year in which the case is being tried (i.e., the present year);

- YR-1 represents last year (please use the actual year);

- YR-2 represents the year before last (please use the actual year), etc.

Copies of the exhibits and the audio of the 911 telephone call are available online at:

http://bit.ly/1P20Jea
Password: Dixon7

STIPULATIONS

1. Nita City has approximately 80,000 residents; Darrow County has approximately 165,000 residents.

2. The height of the desktop in Judge Dixon's office is thirty inches.

3. The height of the doorknob in Exhibit 21 is thirty-six inches.

4. Exhibit 10 is an accurate description and drawing of Judge Dixon's shotgun.

RECOMMENDATIONS FOR FULL TRIALS

When this case file is used for a full bench or jury trial, the following witnesses may be called:

Plaintiff   Mary Dixon

                   Sheriff Altair Khouri

                   Anna Martin

                   Dr. Celli

                   Sarah Lawton (Plaintiff may read Lawton's deposition into evidence instead of calling her as a witness.)

Defendant   Robert Wilson

                   Morgan Crowe

                   Carter Berman

                   Dr. Upchurch

Timeline of Key Events

YR-3

9/15	Dixon withdraws $100,000 from mutual fund.
12/1	Sarah Lawton reimburses state for fines and fees owed by the court.

YR-2

8/8	Dixon withdraws $125,000 from mutual fund; invests in Green By Green.
9/17	Berman writes to Dixon.
10/23	Berman writes to Dixon again.
10/26	Dixon applies for Providential policy.
11/2	Providential policy issued.
11/11	Dixon's death.
11/12	Scheduled meeting between Dixon and Berman.
12/24	Tracy Lawton dies.

YR-1

1/22	Providential denies Mrs. Dixon's claim.
3/2	Mrs. Dixon files suit.
4/1	Sarah Lawton is sentenced for embezzlement.

IN THE CIRCUIT COURT OF
DARROW COUNTY, NITA
CIVIL DIVISION

MARY L. DIXON,	)	
	)	
Plaintiff,	)	
	)	
vs.	)	COMPLAINT
	)	
PROVIDENTIAL LIFE	)	
INSURANCE COMPANY,	)	
	)	
Defendant.	)	

The plaintiff for her complaint against the defendant alleges:

FIRST CLAIM FOR RELIEF

1. At all times relevant to this case, the plaintiff was, and still is, a resident of Darrow County, Nita.

2. The defendant was, and still is, a corporation engaged in the business of writing life insurance contracts in the State of Nita.

3. On or about November 2, YR-2, in consideration of a premium paid by John J. Dixon, the defendant issued a life insurance policy No. 712089 in which the defendant insured the life of John J. Dixon and agreed to pay the beneficiary named in the policy the sum of $1,000,000 upon his death.

4. On or about November 11, YR-2, the insured, John J. Dixon, died.

5. The plaintiff, Mary L. Dixon, is the widow of the insured and is named in policy No. 712089 as the beneficiary.

6. Life insurance policy No. 712089 was in full force and effect on the 11th day of November, YR-2, and the plaintiff has performed all conditions precedent required by the policy.

7. The defendant refuses to pay the plaintiff the sum of $1 million as required by the terms of the life insurance contract upon the death of the insured.

WHEREFORE, the plaintiff demands judgment against the defendant in the sum of $1 million together with interest and costs, for her first claim for relief.

SECOND CLAIM FOR RELIEF

8. The plaintiff realleges paragraphs 1 through 7.

9. Life insurance policy No. 712089 provided for the payment of $1 million to the beneficiary in addition to the face amount of said policy upon the accidental death of the insured.

10. On or about November 11, YR-2, the insured, John J. Dixon, sustained an accidental injury that resulted in his death on or about November 11, YR-2.

11. The defendant refuses to pay the plaintiff the sum of $1 million as required by the terms of the life insurance contract upon the accidental death of the insured.

WHEREFORE, the plaintiff demands judgment against the defendant in the sum of $1 million, together with interest and costs, for her second claim for relief.

JURY DEMAND

The plaintiff demands a trial by jury in this action.

MADDEN & WILLIAMS by

Margaret Dixue

Attorneys for Plaintiff
401 Court Place
Nita City, Nita 99995
(721) 555-4490

DATED: March 2, YR-1

IN THE CIRCUIT COURT OF
DARROW COUNTY, NITA
CIVIL DIVISION

MARY L. DIXON,	)	
	)	
Plaintiff,	)	
	)	
vs.	)	ANSWER
	)	
PROVIDENTIAL LIFE	)	
INSURANCE COMPANY,	)	
	)	
Defendant.	)	

The defendant for its answer to the plaintiff's complaint states:

I.

That the plaintiff's complaint fails to state a claim upon which relief can be granted.

II.

1. Admits the allegations contained in paragraphs 1–5, 9.

2. Denies the allegations contained in paragraphs 6, 7, 10, 11.

3. Life insurance policy No. 712089 provides in relevant part:

    4. SUICIDE OF INSURED—If, within two years from the date of delivery of this policy, the Insured shall die by his own hand or act, the liability of the Company shall not exceed the amount of the premiums theretofore paid on this policy.

4. Life insurance policy No. 712089 was issued and delivered to John J. Dixon on November 2, YR-2.

5. The insured, John J. Dixon, died by his own hand or act on November 11, YR-2.

6. John J. Dixon obtained life insurance policy No. 712089 by fraud and deceit.

7. Providential Life Insurance Company has tendered payment of the premium paid as provided in policy No. 712089 and has performed all its obligations under the life insurance contract.

WHEREFORE, the defendant demands that the complaint be dismissed and judgment entered in favor of the defendant with the costs and disbursements of this action.

BARRETT & SHAFFER

by

Thomas Terwilliger

Attorneys for Defendant
Suite 600, Nita Bank Building
Nita City, Nita 99990
(721) 555-3000

DATED: March 21, YR-1

DEPOSITIONS

DEPOSITION OF SHERIFF ALTAIR KHOURI
JUNE 15, YR-1

1 My name is Altair Khouri. Everyone calls me Al. I live at 254 Maple Street, Nita City. I am the
2 Sheriff of Darrow County. I have been in this position since YR-8. Before being sheriff, I was a
3 deputy for five and a half years. I have a degree in administration of justice from the College
4 of Nita, a two-year program. There are currently fifty deputies in our department. As a deputy
5 sheriff, I trained at the state police academy, and took a two-month accident investigation
6 course at Northwestern University. I also attended a series of lectures and demonstrations for
7 police officers and coroners conducted by the Nita Medical School and the Nita State Police.
8 I have taught a course on crime scene investigation at the state police academy for the past
9 five years.
10
11 I knew John Dixon. He was a lawyer in Nita City for many years, and a county circuit court judge
12 for the past ten years. He was initially appointed by the governor to fill a vacancy when the last
13 circuit judge died, and then he was elected without opposition. We were friends for many years.
14 I also consider Mrs. Dixon a good friend; my wife and I socialized with the Dixons many times.
15
16 On November 11, YR-2, at about 9:45 a.m., I got a call from dispatch that Mary Dixon had
17 called 911 because her husband had accidently shot himself. She said that he was not
18 breathing. Yes, Exhibit 33 is the transcript of that call. An ambulance and patrol car were on
19 their way. As sheriff, I am assigned to cover all of the county outside the city limits. The Dixon
20 house is on Ridge Road; about a quarter of a mile or so outside the city limits and within my
21 jurisdiction. Because of Judge Dixon's position, and because of our friendship, I immediately
22 went to the house. On the way, I called Dr. Celli, the medical examiner, to make sure that
23 Dr. Celli personally went to the scene as well.
24
25 I got to the Dixons' home at about 9:55 a.m. An ambulance and patrol car were out front. Judge
26 Dixon's car, a Chevy, was also parked out front. I saw Mrs. Dixon's car, a Honda, in the garage.
27 I entered the house through the front door, which was open. Mrs. Dixon was in the living
28 room with a neighbor, Mrs. Fisher, who was trying to comfort her. Mrs. Dixon told me that the
29 responders were with John in the study.
30
31 I had often visited the Dixon home, and I was familiar with it. The living room, dining room,
32 and kitchen are on the first floor, and Judge Dixon's study is located near the front entrance,
33 up a half flight of stairs. The study actually sits on top of the garage. It is about twelve by
34 sixteen feet and has a built-in desk on the south wall. A window on the north wall, across
35 from the desk, faces the street, with another window on the west wall.
36
37 When I got to the landing, I saw Judge Dixon's body in front of his desk. He was lying on his
38 back, with his head pointed toward the door and his arms stretched out. The left side of his
39 forehead and the left eye were shot away, with blood over the left side of his face. I entered
40 the office, following standard police protocols for preserving a crime scene. It looked to me
41 as if the wound or wounds had been caused by a blast of a shotgun. The left front of the

1 head was torn off. I observed some sooting in the wound area—gunpowder residue—which
2 indicates that Judge Dixon was shot at close range, less than a foot. This was consistent with
3 the size of the wound.
4
5 When I first observed the body, I noticed a screwdriver, about seven inches long, lying on the
6 floor about eight inches from Judge Dixon's right hand.
7
8 I closed the office door partway to see the other side of it. Tissue blown from the head
9 spattered over the inside of the door, about four to five feet from the floor. It covered an area
10 of about two or three feet. The top of his head was three to four feet from the door.
11
12 Lying along the left side of the body was John's Browning shotgun. The butt or stock of the
13 shotgun was toward his feet. The muzzle of the shotgun was about level with the chest. I mean
14 that the shotgun was lying on the floor and was about parallel with the body, but the stock or
15 butt of the gun was a little farther out. I examined the jacket he was wearing, and found two
16 twelve-gauge shotgun shells in the jacket pocket.
17
18 Later, when I picked up the shotgun from beside the body, I "broke" it—that is, I opened it up.
19 I found a discharged shell in the chamber. The barrel was dirty, but it wasn't real dirty. I saw
20 specks of dirt and powder in the barrel. These particles were loose and not caked on, and
21 there was no buildup of particles. This indicates that the shotgun had been fired only once or
22 twice since it was last cleaned. No, I don't know for sure when it was last cleaned. I imagine
23 Judge Dixon cleaned it that morning before he died. I saw cleaning materials on the desk chair.
24 He was always cleaning and taking care of that gun; it was his favorite. He had his hunting
25 clothes on; we were going hunting together that day. My theory is that he had cleaned the gun
26 and gotten it all ready for the hunting trip, and when he set it down, it accidentally went off.
27
28 When I was in Judge Dixon's office on November 11, I took possession of the shotgun. Before
29 that, the deputies took photos of the scene. Dr. Celli arrived about ten minutes after I did. When
30 we left the study that morning, Dr. Celli went in the ambulance with Judge Dixon's body to the
31 morgue, and I took the shotgun and the other evidence we found at the scene to my office.
32
33 The shotgun that was lying next to Judge Dixon was his twelve-gauge Browning B-SS28. I had
34 it dusted for prints and tested in our forensics lab. The only prints on the gun were John's. The
35 gun was in good working condition.
36
37 There is a safety device on top of the stock of the gun, just behind the device that breaks the
38 gun—where you break the gun to load it. During the past five years, Judge Dixon and I went
39 hunting four or five times a year, sometimes more, every season. He always used the Browning,
40 so I was quite familiar with it. I had handled it, and had seen him fire it. You have to pull the
41 safety device back before the gun can be fired. Based on my observations of his hunting and
42 my tests, I would estimate that the trigger of the gun had about a seven-pound pull.
43
44 After they dusted and tested it, our forensics officer gave the shotgun to the property room
45 clerk and told her to mark it as evidence.

1 I checked the gun at the scene, and I remember that the safety was off. That indicated to me
2 that John thought the gun was unloaded, because he was always very careful with a loaded
3 gun. Whenever we hunted together, he always kept the safety on when it was loaded, even
4 when we were actively hunting and close to game. When he saw a deer or pheasant and was
5 ready to shoot, he would flip the safety off right before or as he was taking aim. It was one
6 of those sliding safeties near the trigger, so he could flip it off and on quite easily. He was a
7 master with that gun—he could flip the safety off, take aim, and fire as quickly and accurately
8 as any hunter I know.
9
10 John was an experienced hunter. The sheriff's deputies have a trap-shooting club, and John
11 was an honorary member. He often took part in our contests. We all used guns provided by
12 the club. Very often he won the prize. I considered John an expert in handling all kinds of
13 guns. A few years ago at one of our club contests, he won a fifty-dollar bet from me in a pistol-
14 shooting contest; he was an excellent marksman and hunter. He knew as much about guns as
15 anybody I've ever met.
16
17   Q: When did you last speak to Judge Dixon before his death?
18
19   A: About a week before. John and I made plans to go hunting that day, November 11.
20   We agreed to meet at noon at my place.
21
22   Q: Did you discuss any details about that arrangement?
23
24   A: I recall asking him which gun he was taking. He said he'd bring his Browning,
25   which surprised me.
26
27   Q: Why did it surprise you?
28
29   A: Because in September YR-2, we were hunting the woods north of town and he
30   was using the Browning, which was his favorite. John went ahead of me, and I
31   couldn't see him. He was out of my sight when I heard a shot. I ran to catch up
32   with John, and he told me that his shotgun had discharged accidentally and that
33   this had happened to him once before with this same gun. On another hunting
34   trip two weeks later, John and I were walking down a trail together, each carrying
35   our guns at our sides. Suddenly, John's gun discharged, and he was so frightened
36   by it he was speechless for several minutes. We checked his gun together and
37   saw that the safety was on.
38
39   Q: Did you ask him why he was taking the Browning, given the problems he'd had
40   with it?
41
42   A: No, I don't recall anything like that.
43
44 Like I said, when I observed his body in the study, I saw the Browning lying next to him. I also
45 saw a screwdriver on the floor near Judge Dixon's right hand. I assume he was using it to fix

1   the gun. He was wearing a big brown leather jacket that wasn't completely zipped up and
2   brown corduroy trousers. He always wore that jacket when we went hunting together. He was
3   wearing heavy brown shoes, the kind he wore when we went out hunting together. In other
4   words, when I saw his body there on the floor of his office on November 11, he was dressed
5   to go hunting with me as we had planned.
6
7   During my observations of Judge Dixon's office on November 11, I did look around for a
8   suicide note. I did not find any. No, I didn't suspect suicide—that's my standard procedure
9   in this sort of situation. In my experience, persons who commit suicide usually leave some
10 note of explanation. I looked around on the top of the desk. I did see some papers on it. In an
11 ashtray on the desk, I did see some ashes and a few fragments of charred paper. As I picked
12 up the ashtray, the fragments crumbled. But I did see something on one of the fragments that
13 looked like handwriting. I could not tell what it was because the fragments of paper crumbled
14 into dust or ash when I touched them. No, I didn't keep the ashes or submit them for testing.
15
16 There was also a sheet of paper with some kind of symbol on it. Yes, you can see it in Exhibit 25.
17 I guess it could be the letter M, but I really can't say for sure. I don't know whether it's in
18 John's handwriting. No, I didn't keep it or have it analyzed.
19
20 There was no sign of disturbance of the furniture in the office. Nothing was out of place. No
21 chairs overturned. No sign of any disorder. No sign of struggle or fight. The door to the office
22 had a push-button lock in the doorknob, but it was open and unlocked when we arrived.
23 There were papers strewn on the desk. I recall seeing a printout of something about a "Green"
24 company, but I didn't really read or take possession of it because it didn't seem important.
25
26 Before I left the Dixon house that day, I talked to Mrs. Dixon. She said she gone to a dentist
27 appointment at 8:30 a.m. She returned home about 9:30 and called to Judge Dixon when she
28 went into the house. When he did not answer, she went to the door to the office and found
29 it locked. She said she got a key in the kitchen, opened the door and went in and found her
30 husband on the floor, dead. She said she disturbed nothing in the room except to open the
31 blinds and replace the telephone, which had been lying on the desk, out of its cradle. She
32 used that phone to call 911.
33
34 So far as I knew, Judge Dixon was in excellent health. He was six feet tall and weighed about
35 200 pounds. He had a great temperament. I never saw him moody or depressed. He was
36 popular in our county as a lawyer and then as a judge. He was a member of the school
37 board and very active in our church, the United Church of the Word of the Almighty. It's an
38 evangelical Christian church that believes that the Bible contains the words of our Lord. He
39 was a very religious man, a member of the vestry, and he and I were ushers at services. I never
40 knew him to miss a Sunday service. I saw him there on the Sunday before he died.
41
42 No, I didn't think we were dealing with a crime scene. The room and the gun were dusted
43 for fingerprints because that is standard practice. We found fingerprints in the study of John,
44 Mary, John's sister-in-law, the Dixon's cleaning lady, and two people whose prints we could
45 not identify.

1   I did not attempt to determine what was stored on John's computer, but I know that John's
2   sister-in-law, Anna, did later that day. The only evidence I seized was the shotgun. No, as I said,
3   I did not believe John had committed suicide. All the evidence at the scene was consistent
4   with a terrible accident. No, I did not consider murder. Nothing pointed in that direction. Yes,
5   those are my professional opinions as a longtime peace officer and as someone who knew
6   John Dixon very well. Yes, I'm aware that Mary Dixon is claiming $2 million in this lawsuit, but
7   that has nothing to do with my opinions.
8
9   Exhibit 34 is the last contact I had with John and there's nothing in that text exchange that
10   indicates that anything was wrong. I assumed that he'd found the problem with his shotgun
11   and planned to use it the next day. No, I don't know what he wanted to discuss with me.

I have read the foregoing transcript of my deposition on the date above and find it is a true and accurate representation of my testimony.

Signed this 27th day of June, YR-1 in Nita City, Nita.

Altair Khouri
Altair Khouri

DEPOSITION OF DR. EMERY CELLI
JUNE 15, YR-1

1   My name is Emery S. Celli, MD. I live at 140 Oakdale Drive in Nita City, Nita. I have been
2   the Darrow County Medical Examiner for the last ten years. This is a part-time, appointed
3   position. In addition, I am permitted to carry on my private practice as a family doctor.
4
5   On November 11, YR-2, at about 9:45 a.m. or so, Sheriff Altair Khouri called me and said
6   that Judge Dixon had shot himself at home and asked me to go to the scene. Al mentioned
7   something about hunting and the judge's shotgun, and so I assumed that a terrible accident
8   had occurred. When I arrived about 10:00 a.m., Mrs. Dixon told me to go into John's study.
9
10 The door to the study is on the east wall. The office has a large window in the front that faces
11 north, towards Ridge Road, and another window facing west. When we entered, the blinds
12 on both windows were open and the overhead lights were on. There is a built-in desk and
13 counter on the south wall.
14
15 In front of the desk, I saw Judge Dixon's body lying face up, with his head pointed toward
16 the door. The left side of the body was about two feet from the desk, almost parallel to it.
17 Both arms extended straight out from the body. The desk chair was pushed against the west
18 wall. I remember thinking that was a bit strange. A shotgun cleaning kit rested on the chair.
19
20 I saw a Browning shotgun, his hunting gun, lying alongside the body. The gun was about a foot
21 from the left side of the body. The stock or butt of the gun was near the feet. The muzzle of
22 the gun was lying on the floor parallel with the left side of the body.
23
24 It was immediately clear that Judge Dixon was dead. His left eye and part of his left forehead
25 were torn off. I observed sooting on the skin of the left forehead in front of the left ear. It
26 appeared that the wound and sooting were caused by the discharge of a shotgun at close range.
27
28 Blood and tissue blown from the head were spattered over the inside of the door, about five
29 feet up from the floor.
30
31 Al Khouri's examinations and observations were made independently of mine. Al examined
32 the gun. We did discuss these observations and conclusions. The gun was a shotgun, and
33 Al told me a discharged shell was found in the chamber of the shotgun. Al believed that
34 the shot that caused Judge Dixon's death was fired upwards. I concur in this opinion.
35 I would agree with Al's conclusion that the wounds I have told you about were received
36 from the front.
37
38 I observed a screwdriver on the floor of the office. It was about six inches long, and it was
39 lying to Judge Dixon's right.

1   Judge Dixon wore hunting clothes—a brown jacket, I think, and dark pants. He was not
2   wearing a hat or cap. He also wore boots of some sort. Judge Dixon looked dressed for the
3   outdoors at the time of his death.

4

5   I had known Judge and Mrs. Dixon for some years. We were friends, and I was also their family
6   physician. So I had both a professional and a private relationship with him. He regularly came
7   to my office every year or two for a physical examination. Yes, I have a copy of the HIPAA
8   authorization signed by Mrs. Dixon that you gave me.

9

10   According to my records, John's last visit to my office was in August of YR-2, when I gave him
11   a complete physical examination. I looked over my records yesterday, and they indicate that I
12   found him to be in excellent health. Judge Dixon was fifty years old. He was about six feet tall
13   and weighed about 200 pounds. His blood pressure was good. His labs were all normal, except
14   for his LDL cholesterol, which was 151—a little high. He had never been a smoker. He hated
15   even the smell of tobacco. No, he never complained of depression or any emotional problems.

16

17   Based on my close acquaintance with him over the years and on observations I made when
18   I gave him his physical examinations, I can positively state that he was never moody or
19   depressed. I never observed any signs of despondency or depression.

20

21   Judge Dixon had an excellent reputation as a practicing lawyer, before he took the bench.
22   I consulted with him on several occasions; in fact, he handled the purchase of my present
23   home some years ago. He also advised me on my professional corporation, and from time to
24   time, he answered some income tax questions I had. I knew him well, both professionally and
25   socially. He was a member of the Board of Education of our county.

26

27   I saw him the day before his death. It was sometime early in the morning that day in downtown
28   Nita City. I met him by chance in the street there. We chatted for about five minutes, just
29   about the weather and the year's hunting prospects. I noticed nothing out of the ordinary
30   about him.

31

32   I conducted the autopsy on John Dixon's body. My findings were that he died of a shotgun
33   wound to the head. The presence of fouling and burning (powder burns) at the entrance
34   wound establishes that Judge Dixon was shot at close range, not more than several inches.

35

36   It is my professional opinion that Judge Dixon's death was accidental. I base this opinion
37   on my autopsy findings, my investigation at the scene, my ten years' experience as county
38   medical examiner during which I have investigated more than a hundred violent deaths,
39   and on a month-long course in forensic medical investigation of death that I took at the
40   Northwestern University School of Medicine in YR-5. That course focused on investigating
41   death scenes and performing autopsies to determine whether death was accidental,
42   homicide, or suicide.

1   The following facts are important in my opinion:

2

3   A)   Judge Dixon did not leave a suicide note. The overwhelming majority of suicides
4   leave a note or its equivalent (e.g., a recording, video, etc.).

5

6   B)   Judge Dixon would have never killed himself the way he did and then leave it for
7   his wife to find him.

8

9   C)   Judge Dixon had never threatened or even talked about suicide. It is extremely
10   rare for someone to commit suicide without having talked about it before.

11

12   D)   Judge Dixon was morally opposed to suicide.

13

14   E)   Judge Dixon had no history of depression or other psychiatric disorder.

15

16   F)   Nothing about the scene was inconsistent with accident.

17

18   G)   Nothing about the autopsy was inconsistent with accident.

19

20   H)   Judge Dixon was essentially shot through the eye. I have never seen this or even
21   read about an intentional, self-inflicted act of this sort.

22

23   I)   Judge Dixon had no history of suicide attempts, which constitute a significant risk
24   factor of suicide.

25

26   J)   Judge Dixon had no history of a psychiatric disorder, another significant risk factor
27   for suicide.

28

29   K)   Judge Dixon's strong family, community, and religious ties were significant
30   protective factors against suicide.

31

32   L)   I know of no evidence that points to murder or a motive for murder.

33

34 Based on all these factors, I believe that Judge Dixon died of accidental causes.

35

36 Yes, I was a close friend of John Dixon's. We were both active in political causes, including
37 the successful effort some years ago to pass a ballot proposal prohibiting same-sex marriage
38 and the successful effort to defeat a proposal to permit assisted suicide. John and I both
39 contributed several thousand dollars to each effort. John was strongly pro-life, both in terms
40 of abortions and assisted suicide. He was not in favor of so-called gay rights. He believed
41 homosexuality violated God's laws, and I agreed 100 percent. Yes, we belonged to the same
42 church, the United Church of the Word of the Almighty.

1   I know nothing about John's relationship with Sarah Lawton except that she was John's long-time
2   court clerk. I have never had any reason to suspect that he was unfaithful to Mary with Sarah or
3   anyone else. John was not that kind of person.

I have read the foregoing transcript of my deposition on the date above and find it is a true and accurate representation of my testimony.

Signed this 30th day of June, YR-1 in Nita City, Nita.

Emery S. Celli
Emery S. Celli, MD

Emery S. Celli, MD

140 Oakdale Drive
Nita City, Nita

Education

- BA University of Ohio, YR-28

- MD Michigan State University, YR-24

Post-graduate training

- Residency, Family Practice—Michigan State University, YR-24 to YR-21

- Anatomical Pathology for the Nonpathologist (intensive three-month course focusing on the performance of autopsies)—Michigan State University, YR-18

- Many CME courses in aspects of family medicine (30 hours per year)

- Forensic Medical Investigation of Death—Northwestern University, YR-5

Professional associations

- State Medical Society

- American Medical Association

- National Association of County Coroners

- American Forensic Pathology Association

Board certified in family practice, YR-10

Civic activities

- Darrow County Medical Examiner, YR-10 to present

- Board of Directors, Nita City Boys and Girls Club

- Chair, Advisory Board, Nita City Youth for Christ

- Board of Directors, Nita Right to Life

- Board of Directors, Darrow County Council on the Arts

- Chair, Darrow County United Way Campaign

- Elected Nita City's Person of the Year, YR-3, by Chamber of Commerce

- President, Nita Physicians for Life, YR-8 to YR-6

DEPOSITION OF MARY L. DIXON
JUNE 1, YR-1

1   John and I were born in Darrow County and lived here all our lives. We were married for
2   twenty-four years. We didn't have any children. My husband was an attorney, and he practiced
3   mainly real estate law and handled small business matters and estates until he was appointed
4   judge. He loved being a judge and was extremely well respected. He had an office in the
5   local courthouse and a study in our home that was connected to his courthouse office by
6   computer. I guess everybody in the county knew us.
7
8   John was a member of the State Bar Association, and a member of the bar association's
9   Committee on Judicial Ethics, and a member of the state bar Committee on Circuit Courts. He
10 was also a member of the county board of education. He was very active in our church, the
11 United Church of the Word of the Almighty. He was past-president of the State Conservative
12 Caucus, and the Nita Right to Life board. There were many other civic activities and committees,
13 but I can't remember all the titles.
14
15 My husband was a very religious man. He never missed a Sunday service, and he was very
16 active in church functions. He had served on the vestry for many years.
17
18 On the day after my husband's funeral, I found a life insurance policy among his papers. It
19 was from the Providential Life Insurance Company, and it was dated November 2, YR-2. I am
20 the beneficiary. The policy is for $1 million; if the death is accidental, it doubles to $2 million.
21
22 After I found this policy, I called the insurance company. November 18, I think it was, an
23 insurance agent named Robert Wilson came to my home. I gave him the policy, and then
24 he explained the difference between term and whole life insurance. I gathered from what
25 he said that most people my husband's age usually buy term insurance because it's much
26 less expensive than whole life. Mr. Wilson said that he and my husband discussed this quite
27 extensively in October YR-2, when John contacted the agent about purchasing some insurance.
28 Mr. Wilson said that John decided to purchase the five-year term insurance. Toward the end
29 of October John completed an application, and Providential Life Insurance Company issued
30 the insurance policy on November 2, YR-2.
31
32 After we had talked about the policy, Mr. Wilson asked me to sign some papers for him, which
33 he said were statements of claim. I signed them as he requested. While I was signing, I told
34 him that because my husband's death was accidental, I was entitled to the double amount of
35 $2 million. He didn't really respond to this; all he said was that the company would consider
36 the claim. He told me that I would hear from them, and then he left.
37
38 I didn't hear anything about the insurance policy until I got an email from Mr. Wilson dated
39 January 22, YR-1. A letter from the insurance company was attached to the email. The company
40 refused to pay the policy's full amount. Instead, the letter said Providential was returning the
41 policy with their letter and a $1,219 check to cover the premiums paid.

1   Q: When you received the policy back from Providential, were there any check
2   marks on the left-hand side?
3

4   A: Yes, there were three check marks.
5

6   Q: Were those check marks on the policy when you gave it to Mr. Wilson on
7   November 18?
8

9   A: I don't know. I was so upset about John's death that I wasn't noticing little things
10   like check marks.
11

12 I have no idea who made those check marks. There is no way to tell whether John made them
13 or not. They just look like anybody's check marks to me.
14

15 When Providential returned the policy to me, they said that John had committed suicide and
16 as a result they weren't going to pay me anything beyond returning the premium already paid.
17

18 They sent a check for $1,219, which they said was a refund of the premiums my husband paid.
19 I haven't cashed this check because it says on the back that if I cash it, I release the company
20 from all liability. They say my husband committed suicide. That is not true. His death was
21 accidental. I emailed Mr. Wilson demanding that they pay the $2 million that is rightfully due
22 under the policy or else I would have to sue.
23

24 I didn't know that my husband had this life insurance policy from the Providential Company
25 until I found it among his papers after the funeral. He hadn't mentioned it to me, but he was
26 very busy with his work and he had a lot of things on his mind. No, I don't know the details; he
27 thought it was unethical for him to discuss court cases with me. But I know he had to be at his
28 office in the courthouse lots of nights. Sometimes he didn't get home until after I was asleep.
29

30 In addition to the life insurance policy with the Providential Company, my husband also had
31 a $50,000 life insurance policy that he had purchased right after we were married. It was a
32 whole life insurance policy with double indemnity for accidental death. This policy was issued
33 by New York Life. I found it in John's office. The agent told me the cash value at the time of
34 John's death was $19,500. I got a copy of Dr. Celli's coroner's report, and I filed a claim with
35 the company. They sent me a check for the full amount with double indemnity, $100,000,
36 within a month after I sent in the claim.
37

38 When I was going through John's papers in his office, I also found a life insurance policy that
39 he must have taken out when he first became a judge. It was dated shortly after he became
40 a judge, and the papers with it indicated that he got it through a plan the state courts have
41 for the judges. I guess it was a special group plan, and the premiums were deducted from
42 his salary. The policy said that it was a term life insurance policy, and it was $30,000 with
43 double payment— $60,000—for accidental death. I sent in a notice of claim to that company,
44 in Capitol City, and they paid also. They paid the full amount, double coverage of $60,000,
45 within a month or six weeks after I sent in the claim. Because the policy was over two years

1   old, the company could not rely on the suicide exclusion. Yes, the same was true for the New
2   York Life policy.
3
4   When my husband died, I thought our house on Ridge Road was paid for. I remember about
5   five years ago John said, "Well, there's the last mortgage payment," and we had a little
6   celebration for having the mortgage paid off and now owning the house. After John's death,
7   I discovered that about a year before he died, he had borrowed $100,000 from the First State
8   Bank and that he used the house as collateral or security for the loan. He signed my name on
9   all the papers. The bank called me shortly after his death. They told me not to worry about
10 the loan, because John had obtained credit life insurance on the loan and that would take
11 care of everything. There was no suicide clause in this credit life insurance policy.
12
13 At the time of John's death, my youngest sister, Anna Martin, was living with us. She moved
14 in July YR-2, when she got a position as a math teacher at Mumford High School here. Before
15 that, she taught school in Capitol City. She had broken up with her long-time partner, and she
16 wanted to make a new beginning. John suggested that she move to Nita City and live with us
17 until she found a place of her own.
18
19 On the night before my husband's death, November 10, the three of us had dinner together
20 at 6:30 p.m., as usual. My husband certainly did not act or behave like a man who was going
21 to, or who was planning to, take his own life a few hours later. He was laughing and joking,
22 in good spirits and cheerful during dinner. He even had two glasses of wine instead of his
23 usual one.
24
25 He was certainly not despondent or down. In all our married life—we were married twenty-four
26 years—I never knew him to be glum or subject to moods or depressions; he was the most cheerful
27 man I have ever known. Our married life was a happy one. He was always kind, affectionate, and
28 considerate. The fact that he was so willing to take in my sister is an example of his generosity.
29
30 During dinner that night, I remember he discussed some problem Anna had had in her class
31 that day; she was teaching geometry. He helped her work out the problem.
32
33 While we were at the table, there were a couple of times when I asked him something or other,
34 I don't recall what it was now, but he did not answer me. I had to repeat the question several
35 times. He was sort of distracted or detached, then sort of far away, and when I repeated my
36 question, he said, "I'm sorry, I wasn't paying attention I guess," or something like that. He ate
37 a big dinner.
38
39 As we finished eating, he told me that someone was coming over to get some advice from
40 him on a confidential matter. Yes, that was unusual, but not unheard of. I don't know who it
41 was.
42
43 After dinner, I went up to our bedroom on the second floor to watch TV. The bedroom is a half
44 flight above my husband's study, which is on a landing between the first and second floors of
45 the house. Later on, I heard some discussion from the study. I could not recognize the other

1   voice other than to say it was a man's, nor could I make out what either was saying. It seemed
2   like a pretty intense conversation, but that's all I can say about it. I sort of dozed off during the
3   eleven o'clock news. About 11:30 p.m. my husband came up and woke me. He joked with me
4   about my falling asleep in front of the TV. I asked him what had been going on in his office, but
5   he told me that it was nothing and not to worry about it. We sat and watched the late show
6   on TV for about ten minutes. Then we went to sleep.
7
8   Before we went to sleep, John mentioned that he had an important meeting downtown the
9   next morning and that he planned to go hunting with Al Khouri in the afternoon. It was a
10   court holiday. John was an avid hunter, and he often hunted with Al.
11
12   My husband slept soundly that night, as far as I know. I usually sleep soundly myself, but I
13   woke up a couple of times during the night, and heard his slow, regular breathing. The last
14   time I woke up was around 4:00 a.m., and he was sleeping soundly then.
15
16   When I got up at around 7:00, John was already out of bed. That was not unusual; he was always
17   an early riser. I dressed and went down to the kitchen at about 7:30. Anna was just leaving for
18   school. She told me that John had come down about 6:15 and that she had offered to prepare
19   his breakfast, but that he had said he would just grab a quick cup of coffee and toast. I remember
20   this because he usually ate a hearty breakfast. Anna said that he sat with her for a few minutes
21   while he finished his coffee and toast and then he went upstairs to his study. She said he told her
22   that he had to prepare for his meeting downtown, and he did not want to be disturbed.
23
24   Anna left for school, and I ate breakfast by myself. At about 8:00, I left for a dentist appointment.
25   I didn't say anything to John because I thought he was busy and I didn't want to disturb him.
26   So the last time I saw him alive was the night before.
27
28   I got back from the dentist's about 9:30 or 9:40. I parked in the garage and went into the
29   house through the garage. I called out to John, but he didn't answer. I tried the door to his
30   office, and it was locked. I rapped at it, but there was no answer. No sound from inside. I was
31   frightened. I don't recall him ever locking the door before. Then I remembered that I had a
32   key to the door in the kitchen. So I ran back and got it, unlocked the door, and went in.
33
34   I saw John lying on the floor on his back. He had both arms stretched out. He was lying in front
35   of the desk. His head was pointed toward the door. There was blood all over his forehead
36   on the left side, I think over his left eye and left side. He was wearing his hunting jacket—a
37   big, bulky leather jacket he always wore when he went out hunting. I had given it to him as a
38   Christmas present. And I saw his hunting gun. It was lying on the floor on his right side. The
39   bottom of the gun was toward his feet. The barrel was about an inch or two from his head. It
40   was all so horrible and shocking. I was stunned. I almost fainted.
41
42   I ran and opened the blinds on the windows. I think the overhead ceiling light was on. I ran
43   over and felt his head, and it was cold. It was a horrible shock. I knew that John was dead.
44   I called 911. I could not stay in the room. I ran across to my neighbor Mrs. Fisher's, and she
45   came back with me to wait for the police.

1   As I told you, John was dressed for his hunting trip with Al Khouri. He had his brown hunting
2   jacket on.
3
4   Al and Dr. Celli also showed up, and they went into the study. Mrs. Fisher had called Anna at
5   school, and she came home shortly after Al and Dr. Celli arrived. Dr. Celli said they would have
6   to take his body to the county morgue for an autopsy and that the morgue would call the
7   funeral home and have them make arrangements.
8
9   When I went into the study, I did not touch the gun. I didn't touch any object in the room
10   except to pull the blinds open and to pick up the phone, which was off the cradle, to call 911.
11   Did I put the phone back on the cradle after I called 911? Probably. So when the police and
12   Dr. Celli and Al Khouri got there, the study was in the same condition as when I entered, other
13   than those two particulars. The door to John's study has a push button lock in the handle. If
14   you push the button before or after you close the door, it's locked.
15
16   I don't know anything about guns. All I know was that it was a shotgun that he used for
17   hunting. My husband loved to hunt and fish, but he liked hunting the most. Every chance he
18   got, he would be off with his gun, hunting. He took excellent care of his gun, cleaning and
19   repairing it regularly. My sister, Anna, liked hunting, and she went with John a few times. He
20   hunted most often with Al Khouri.
21
22   My husband once mentioned that he'd had shotguns since his father gave him his first gun
23   and taught him how to use it. John was expertly familiar with guns. I remember once when he
24   was going out hunting with this gun of his, and I said to him, "John, you will be careful, won't
25   you?" and he replied, "Mary, nobody in this county knows more about handling a gun than I
26   do. So don't you worry about me."
27
28   I also remember that in September YR-2, he went hunting in upper Darrow County one time,
29   and I saw him take that particular shotgun with him. When he came home, he said he'd had
30   trouble with it. The gun went off accidentally, and gave him a bad scare. He said, "I think I'll
31   have to buy a new gun," but I don't remember his doing so.
32
33   In October YR-2, John went out hunting alone one time, and when he came back, he told me
34   that he had borrowed a gun from Al Khouri, because he didn't trust his old gun very much.
35
36   John was right-handed. He was fifty at the time of death, and he was in excellent health. He
37   had regular checkups with Dr. Celli. The last time was in August of YR-2.
38
39   I didn't find any sort of a suicide note or any message or indication for me. It is unbelievable that
40   John would take his own life. He believed that taking any life, even one's own, was a grave sin.
41   That's why he was so opposed to abortion. Yes, he was opposed to capital punishment as well.
42
43   No, John had never attempted or threatened suicide. The only family history of suicide was that
44   his mother's brother had killed himself when he was in high school. No, I don't know anything
45   more about it. John never told me anything about it; I learned of it from John's mother.

1 John died without a will; isn't that just like an attorney? I was appointed personal representative
2 of his estate. Frank Jackson is the attorney for the estate. I went over my husband's accounts
3 and papers and discovered that at the time of his death, he had $1,200 in our checking account
4 and $2,500 in our savings account. We kept most of our savings in a mutual fund. We'd had
5 about $250,000 in the account, but I discovered that John had withdrawn $100,000 from it
6 in September YR-3, and another $125,000 on August 8, YR-2. No, I didn't know about either
7 withdrawal, and I still don't know why he did it. John also had a 401(k) retirement account
8 with about $120,000 in it. The house and property are valued at $325,000.
9
10 In going over John's papers, I found that in August YR-2, he had invested $125,000 in a hedge fund
11 that specialized in carbon future derivatives, whatever they are. When I checked out the fund, I
12 learned that shortly before John's death it went bust and that the CEO has been indicted for fraud.
13
14 When I was going over the papers in John's office after his death, I found a letter from
15 someone named Berman who was with the attorney general's office. I also found a copy of
16 a letter my husband apparently had sent to Berman. No, he never said anything about this
17 to me. Sarah Lawton had worked for the court since before John became a judge. We both
18 thought highly of her, and I was shocked to read that she had embezzled money from the
19 county. No, we had never socialized with her except at court functions. No, I had never met
20 anyone in her family.
21
22 John's home computer was a laptop. Yes, Anna and I used it after his death, but a few months
23 later it got hit with a bad virus and we had to get rid of it. No, I never searched it after his
24 death, but I now know that Anna did.
25
26 Yes, I saw the Green By Green papers on his desk after he died. I had no idea what they were,
27 and eventually I threw them out. I also saw the paper with some kind of scratching on it that's
28 shown on Exhibit 25. No, it doesn't look like the letter "M" to me or like John's handwriting.
29 I don't know who wrote it or anything about it.
30
31 No, I never had any reason to think that John was unfaithful to me. It's really insulting to his
32 memory that you'd even bring it up.
33
34 I am employed as a librarian at the county library. I work about twenty-five hours a week. I've
35 had that job for about ten years. I was scheduled to work from noon to five on the day John died.

I have read the foregoing transcript of my deposition on the date above and find it is a true
and accurate representation of my testimony.

Signed this 17th day of June, YR-1 in Nita City, Nita.

Mary L. Dixon
Mary L. Dixon

DEPOSITION OF ROBERT L. WILSON
APRIL 20, YR-1

1 My name is Robert L. Wilson. I live at 7546 Marion Avenue in Nita City. I have been general
2 manager of Providential Life Insurance Company's Nita City office since YR-11. One of my
3 duties is supervising claims. I knew Judge Dixon for about five years.
4
5 Around the middle of October YR-2, Judge Dixon called me and said he was thinking about
6 purchasing additional life insurance. We set up an appointment for October 19. We met at
7 my office, where I outlined the various plans and the realistic options available to a man of his
8 age. I had prepared a life insurance profile (Exhibit 1) for him, and we discussed the various
9 plans and the costs. I explained the features of the various plans, and he ultimately decided
10 on the yearly renewable term. During our discussion, he seemed his usual self. He exhibited
11 the typical concern of a man his age about his wife's financial security. It is customary to ask
12 a client why he is obtaining insurance. Judge Dixon said that he was getting older, and he
13 wanted to make sure he had sufficient protection for his wife in case anything should happen
14 to him. At that time, he did not indicate anything was wrong or that he was in any trouble.
15
16 Judge Dixon decided on the term policy, and he came in and signed the application on October 26.
17 I immediately processed the application, and on November 2, YR-2, the company issued the
18 $1 million term policy with waiver of premiums and accidental death benefits to Judge Dixon.
19 I deposited Judge Dixon's check for the annual premium of $1,219 on the issuing date.
20
21 Judge Dixon was found dead in his home on November 11, YR-2, killed by a shotgun blast.
22 A shotgun was found lying next to him; it was his hunting gun.
23
24 The beneficiary of the policy, his widow, Mary L. Dixon, made a claim on the policy. I received
25 the claim on November 18 and referred it to the claims department for investigation. Our
26 investigation revealed suicide as cause of death, and we denied the claim under the terms of
27 the policy. The decision to deny the accidental death claim was made on facts surrounding
28 the death, which indicated suicide. There also were indications that Judge Dixon had serious
29 financial difficulties and was involved in an investigation by the state attorney general's office.
30
31 Yes, murder would come within the accidental death clause, but there was no evidence
32 whatsoever that pointed to murder.
33
34 On January 22, I emailed Mrs. Dixon, attaching a letter informing her that the company denied
35 liability under the policy and would refund the premiums paid. In this letter, I explained that
36 the company's investigation showed that the insured committed suicide within two years
37 from the date of issuance of the policy; therefore, our only liability under the terms of the
38 policy was to refund the premiums paid in the amount of $1,219. I also sent a physical copy
39 of the letter, in which I enclosed our check for $1,219. Mrs. Dixon replied with an email dated
40 January 25 stating that she refused to cash the check for the premium, and she threatened
41 to sue us.

1   In its investigation, our claims department reviewed the autopsy report and spoke with
2   Sheriff Khouri and Dr. Celli. They also noted that Dr. Celli and Sheriff Khouri were good friends
3   of Judge Dixon. During the investigation, they discovered that the attorney general's office
4   was investigating Judge Dixon's court clerk in regard to fines and fees collected by the court.
5   One of our agents met with Carter Berman, chief of the audit and investigations division of
6   the attorney general's office, and obtained copies of correspondence between Berman and
7   Judge Dixon.
8
9   Morgan Crowe is a stockbroker with offices in our building who I know both professionally
10   and socially. We see each other occasionally in the building, at Rotary meetings, and we've
11   gotten together on social occasions. He has bought and sold stocks for me. I met him in
12   the building one day not long after Judge Dixon's death, and we talked about it. Mr. Crowe
13   mentioned that Judge Dixon had a substantial financial loss shortly before his death and that
14   he was trying to raise some money. The way Mr. Crowe told it, it sounded as if Judge Dixon
15   was in dire need of money at the time of his death. Yes, Exhibit 14 is an email I sent to Morgan
16   regarding that discussion.
17
18   Sometime after Judge Dixon's death, Mrs. Dixon called me at my office. At her request, I went
19   to her home on November 18. At that time, she turned the policy over to me and also signed
20   proofs of death and claims. She demanded that we pay $2 million and asserted that her
21   husband's death was accidental. I said we would look into the matter.
22

23   Q: Did you examine the policy when Mrs. Dixon gave it to you on November 18?
24
25   A: I can't say that I "examined" it. I might have glanced at it while I was putting it into
26   my briefcase.
27
28   Q: So you don't recall seeing any check marks at that time?
29
30   A: No, not at that time, but where else could they have come from if not Judge
31   Dixon himself?
32

33   When I got it back to my office, I gave the policy to my assistant, Susan Waterman. I asked her
34   to review the policy and Mrs. Dixon's claim documents. A day or two later, Susan brought the
35   policy back to me and asked me about the check marks and whether I had put them on the
36   policy. I told her that I absolutely had not.
37

38   We think the check marks are quite significant. It looks as if Judge Dixon carefully considered
39   the policy's provisions, and then took his own life—but arranged the event to appear
40   accidental. Note that this check mark appears in the margin opposite the provisions dealing
41   with accidental death, suicide, etc. I can't imagine that they were on the policy when we
42   issued it.
43

44   I had met Judge Dixon many times in the course of business and at social affairs. I last saw
45   him in my office on November 10, YR-2, at about 2:30 p.m. We met by appointment that day.

1   He asked me whether the policy had any loan value, whether he could borrow on it. He said
2   he wanted to borrow at least $100,000. He said he desperately needed this amount by noon
3   the next day. He had the policy with him, and he handed it to me. I can positively state that
4   the marks I showed you on the margin of the policy were not on it at the time. I can only
5   conclude that Judge Dixon put them on the policy later.
6
7   I understand Mrs. Dixon found him at about 9:30 a.m. on November 11, lying on the floor
8   of his study. He was in front of his desk with his hunting gun lying beside him. Of course,
9   she claims his death was an accident; that the gun discharged accidentally. We just cannot
10 see how the death of the judge can be found accidental. If it was not accidental, there is no
11 alternative other than the conclusion that he took his own life.
12
13 Like I said, on the afternoon of November 10, when he came to see me about borrowing
14 $100,000 on the policy, he had the policy with him. When he said he was desperate for money
15 by the next day and wanted to borrow on the policy, I looked over the policy just to satisfy him.
16 I was surprised that as an attorney he would not know that term insurance has no loan value. I
17 informed Judge Dixon that the company would not and could not loan him anything on his policy.
18
19 I think he stayed for thirty minutes. When he left, he shook hands with me. He said: "Well,
20 Bob, you were always a good friend over the years. I thank you for it." He said good-bye and
21 left. His face was pale, haggard, and drawn. I can swear that as he left the office, he sort of
22 muttered to himself, but I'm not clear exactly what he said except, "Oh God, oh God." That
23 part I definitely heard.
24
25 It looks as if Judge Dixon kept up a good front to his friends over the years, but behind it he
26 had deep problems and worries, and they finally got to him. The problems were too much for
27 him to handle, and he took the suicide way out. But he was smart enough to try to make it
28 look like an accidental death so that his widow would get $2 million. We, of course, feel sorry
29 for Mrs. Dixon, but we owe it to our stockholders not to pay claims like this one. The facts and
30 physical evidence show it was a suicide.
31
32 The last time I saw John before November 10 was about two weeks earlier, I can't remember
33 the exact date. I had a late lunch with a client at Rick's Restaurant downtown, and I saw John
34 there with a scruffy looking young man. John introduced me to him as Tracy Lawton, Sarah
35 Lawton's son. I must say that Tracy seemed quite unfriendly, even sullen.
36
37 Yes, I know Sarah pretty well. I'd sold policies to her and her late husband, and I knew that
38 she was John's clerk and maybe more. By that I mean that they might have had a romantic
39 relationship. I base that on the fact that about two years before John's death, I saw the two of
40 them at a restaurant in Capitol City. It was during the State Bar convention where Providential
41 had a booth for the products we provide for lawyers. I had a late dinner with some potential
42 customers and as I was leaving I saw John and Sarah. They seemed to be having an intense
43 conversation so I didn't bother them. No, I don't know if they saw me. Yes, I'm sure it was
44 John and Sarah. I thought it was pretty unusual that he was with her at 10:00 at night, more
45 than 100 miles from Nita City. And even more so that he was holding her hand.

I have read the foregoing transcript of my deposition on the date above and find it is a true and accurate representation of my testimony.

Signed this 12th day of May, YR-1 in Nita City, Nita.

Robert L. Wilson

Robert L. Wilson

DEPOSITION OF ANNA MARTIN
JUNE 12, YR-1

1   My name is Anna Martin. I am Mary Dixon's sister. I was the baby of the family, and Mary
2   was always like a second mother to me. I am twenty-seven years old. I graduated from Nita
3   University and taught school for three years in Capitol City.

4

5   In YR-2, I decided to move to Nita City because I had just gone through a painful breakup with
6   my long-time partner, and I felt like I needed a new start. I got a teaching job at Mumford High
7   School. John suggested that I move in with him and Mary until I could find a place of my own
8   that I really liked.

9

10 Although I only lived with my sister and her husband for a brief period, I found their
11 relationship to be very close and mature. John Dixon was an extraordinary man, both as an
12 individual and as a citizen. He was very sensitive and pleasant and extremely well-liked by
13 everyone.

14

15 John was also a deeply religious man. He belonged to the United Church of the Word of the
16 Almighty, where he was a vestryman. No, I don't belong to that church, and I don't necessarily
17 agree with its precepts. But any suggestion that John Dixon took his own life would be totally
18 out of character for him and his beliefs.

19

20 On the evening of November 10, YR-2, I had dinner with John and Mary. John was in high
21 spirits, often joking with Mary and me. He also mentioned that he planned to go hunting the
22 following day at noon with Al Khouri.

23

24 I hunted with John on occasion. One time in particular was in September YR-2. I remember
25 that time because we had trouble with the shotgun. At one point, I took aim with the gun and
26 attempted to fire it, but the gun would not discharge. I remember John saying he had had
27 trouble with his shotgun before.

28

29 After dinner on the evening of November 10, YR-2, John told me that someone was coming
30 over later to discuss an important matter. No, he didn't tell me anything else about his
31 appointment. I went out for a beer with one of my teacher friends, and I returned about
32 10:30. Driving up, I saw that the light was on in John's study, and the blinds were closed. When
33 I got into the house I went up to John's study and knocked on his door. He said, "Come in," but
34 when I tried the door it was locked. Yes, that was very unusual; John never locked his study
35 door.

36

37 When John opened the door, he said he had forgotten that the door was locked. We just
38 chatted for a minute or two. No, nothing seemed unusual except for the locked door and
39 the fact that John's shotgun was on his desk. Then I remembered that he and Al Khouri were
40 going hunting the next day, so I didn't give it any further thought.

1   I had breakfast with John at 6:30 the next morning, and then I left for school. John seemed
2   fine. I was called to the principal's office, where I was informed of the accident. I am sure it
3   was an accident. John was a good and kind man, and it is absurd to suggest that he committed
4   suicide. He would never have shot himself in the head to begin with, and certainly would
5   never have done it where Mary would find him.
6
7   I couldn't believe what happened to John, nothing made any sense. So the next day I looked
8   into his computer. It was still on the desk in his study. No, the police did not confiscate it. First,
9   I looked at his browser. I found his history for one day. He'd obviously erased everything older
10   than that. Yes, that's his history, your Exhibit 32. I was surprised to find only one day's history
11   because John was not good with technology, and I doubt that he knew how to erase web
12   search history or even that browsers compiled histories.
13
14   Besides his business email, jdixon@darrowcty.nita, I discovered that he had an email address
15   at jjdix@nita.nita. No, I didn't know anything about it. I asked Mary, and she didn't either. It
16   looked to be a filter email, where he directed spam, but I noticed one thing on it that was out
17   of the ordinary—the exchange that's been marked as Exhibit 30 and the sent mail that's Exhibit
18   31. Everything else seemed to be the usual spam. I had no idea who Tracy was. I emailed this
19   Tracy from my account, but I didn't get any response. No, I didn't send an email from John's
20   account. I don't know why, I just didn't. I tried again a couple of months later, and my email
21   bounced back. No, I didn't try again after that. I assumed that Sarah was Sarah Lawton. No, I
22   never knew that she had a son, Tracy, but I know that now and I know he committed suicide
23   shortly after John's death.
24
25   Yes, I checked John's smart phone. I found nothing out of the ordinary—only the type of
26   apps I expected: weather, the *Wall Street Journal*, Nita Rules of Evidence, the NRA, Google
27   Maps, a word game, a family values app, a right-to-life app, a couple of airline apps, and
28   Flight Tracker. I think that's all of them, but I can't really be sure. No, I didn't open any
29   of them.
30
31   No, I didn't tell Mary anything about what I found in that email account, or the browser
32   history, or the texts. I thought she had enough to deal with. I threw John's phone in the
33   trash. Yes, that was an emotional act, but there you are. No, I wasn't attempting to "destroy
34   evidence" or anything like that. I was just acting out of sorrow. I printed out the computer's
35   browser history, and then I cleared it. I also deleted all of John's emails. Yes, another
36   emotional act. I don't know why I printed the ones I did, but I did. Yes, all that I printed have
37   been marked as exhibits. About six months after John's death, his laptop developed some
38   major problems. I took it to a computer repair guy, who said that it was badly infected by a
39   virus and that as old as it was, it would be cheaper to replace than repair. So I dropped it off
40   at the recycling center.
41
42   I never had any reason to think that John was unfaithful to Mary. They seemed to have a
43   wonderful relationship.

I have read the foregoing transcript of my deposition on the date above and find it is a true and accurate representation of my testimony.

Signed this 1st day in July, YR-1 in Nita City, Nita

Anna Martin

——————————————

Anna Martin

DEPOSITION OF MORGAN F. CROWE
JUNE 14, YR-1

1   My name is Morgan F. Crowe. I live at 403 Birch Street, Nita City. I am a stockbroker with Pine
2   Weaver Investments, whose offices are in the Nita Bank Building in Nita City.
3
4   I understand that Judge Dixon's widow is suing the Providential Life Insurance Company on a
5   life insurance policy. She is claiming her husband's death was an accident and that under the
6   double indemnity policy, the company should pay her $2 million as beneficiary. I've heard the
7   company is claiming it was suicide.
8
9   I knew Judge Dixon. He was a client of mine. But I never met his wife. I also know Robert
10 Wilson at Providential Life, which is located in this building. I am his personal stockbroker.
11 I see him socially, at Rotary functions, and also professionally. I have been working on getting
12 some of Providental's institutional business for some time now.
13
14 I was born in Nita City and went to school here. So I knew Judge Dixon since childhood. He
15 was a lawyer, then a judge, and a member of our school board. In all this time, he enjoyed the
16 reputation in our community as being a man of honesty and integrity. Everybody spoke of him
17 as a good man—kind, generous, and charitable.
18
19 I knew him pretty well. I had business dealings with him for a number of years. He advised me
20 on my income tax returns, even after he became a judge. He also bought and sold his mutual
21 fund shares through me.
22
23 My last transaction with him was in August YR-2. According to my records, on August 8, YR-2,
24 he invested in the Green By Green hedge fund. I didn't know anything about it until John
25 called me and told me he was thinking of investing in it. I looked into it and discovered that
26 it was a very volatile fund involved in the margins of green technology. Its purpose seemed
27 to be quick profits, not sustained growth. The CEO was a guy named Elmo Lassiter, who'd
28 been tried on charges of insider trading a few years back, but acquitted. I recommended
29 against the investment because I thought it was too speculative, but John insisted on it and
30 invested $125,000.
31
32   Q: So you made the investment for him in Green By Green?
33
34   A: Yes, I placed the $125,000 investment for him as a favor.
35
36   Q: Did you receive any commission from the hedge fund in connection with the
37   investment?
38
39   A: Yes, I received a standard 5 percent commission from the fund.

1   No, I don't have anything in writing relating to my recommendation against the investment.
2   Yes, it's company policy to memo a negative recommendation when the client disregards it.
3   I don't know why, but I didn't do it; probably just the press of business.
4
5   When we spoke about this prior to August 8, YR-2, he told me, as I recall, that he had heard
6   about this fund somewhere and wanted to buy into it. I recall he said something like: "I'm
7   in a pretty bad financial squeeze just now, and I'd like to make some money fast. I can make
8   a quick killing on it, and I need the money. I need the money fast." I tried to interest him
9   in a more conservative, safer investment, but he would not take my advice. Unfortunately,
10   I turned out to be right. The fund went bust in late October YR-2, when the feds revealed that
11   it was basically a Ponzi scheme. No, not on the same scale as Bernie Madoff, but the same
12   sort of thing.
13
14   My last contact with John was on the morning of November 11, YR-2. He called my office
15   around 9:00 a.m. I was shocked at the sound of his voice. He sounded frightened and shaky.
16   The tone of his voice alarmed me. I knew something was wrong. In all my previous dealings
17   with him, I never knew him to be moody or depressed. I often met him socially and in
18   community affairs.
19
20   He sounded like a different man during that phone call. His voice sounded so frightened and
21   shaky that I asked, "What's the matter, John? Is there anything wrong with you?" He sounded
22   as if he were in terrible fear that something was going to happen to him right then. He asked
23   me if I could loan him some money. I said, "How much, John?" He said: "I have to have
24   $100,000 by noon. You know I got cleaned out on that hedge fund deal." I was sorry for
25   him. But I couldn't raise $100,000 for him myself by noon. I told him that I just didn't have
26   it. He said: "Morgan, I'm desperate. I don't know what to do. I can't tell you what I need the
27   money for. But I am desperate." He repeated the word "desperate" several times. I asked him
28   why he didn't go to the First Trust Company for a loan. He said he had already had his house
29   mortgaged "up to the hilt" and that the bank would not give him any more.
30
31   I asked him if he had an insurance policy he could borrow on. He said he had one with the
32   Providential Life Insurance Company, but that they had turned him down when he tried to
33   borrow on the policy. He said he had only taken out the policy on November 2, YR-2, and it
34   was too soon to borrow on it. I remember he gave a sort of dull laugh and said, "I'm worth
35   more dead than alive on that policy."
36
37   We only talked about three or four minutes. Finally, just before he hung up, he said: "Well,
38   Morgan, thanks. I'll have to see what I can do somewhere else. You have been a good friend
39   all my life."
40
41   Because of his status in the community, people talked about Judge Dixon's death for months.
42   I remember discussing it with Robert Wilson about a month afterwards, although I'm not
43   sure if it was at one of our regular Rotary meetings or if I just ran into him in our building. I
44   didn't realize Robert was Judge Dixon's insurance agent, but when I told him about my last

1 conversation with Judge Dixon, he became quite interested in what I had to say
2 a copy of an email I received from Robert Wilson right after this conversation.
3
4 Was Judge Dixon the kind of man I thought would take his own life? I can't give you a definite
5 answer. I can only say that no matter how a man appears to others, no one can say with
6 certainty that behind all the outward appearances there may not be something that will, in a
7 moment of despair or depression, induce him to commit suicide. But I know that morally he
8 was opposed to suicide because he was quite active in the campaign to defeat Nita's assisted-
9 suicide ballot proposal. Yes, it was defeated by almost 55 percent to 45 percent.
10
11 No, I don't have an opinion about whether John took his own life. If you asked me the question
12 based solely on what I knew of him before the strange phone conversation of November 11,
13 I'd have to say he wasn't the kind of man you'd expect to commit suicide. I understand I might
14 be the last one who talked to him before he died. I realize how nervous, depressed, and
15 desperate he sounded. So I don't know, maybe he did kill himself, but I really doubt it.

I have read the foregoing transcript of my deposition on the date above and find it is a true
and accurate representation of my testimony.

Signed this 3rd day of July, YR-1 in Nita City, Nita

Morgan F. Crowe
Morgan F. Crowe

DEPOSITION OF CARTER J. BERMAN
OCTOBER 22, YR-1

1   My name is Carter J. Berman. I live at 105 First Avenue, Capitol City, Nita. I am chief of the
2   Audit and Investigations Division of the Office of the Attorney General of Nita. I have been
3   employed for the past five years with the attorney general's office, and I am also a certified
4   public accountant.
5
6   I've heard that Mrs. Dixon is suing the Providential Life Insurance Company on a life insurance
7   policy. As I understand it, she claims her husband's death was an accident, and the insurance
8   company says it was a suicide. Apparently, there is quite a bit of money involved—I've heard
9     $2 million.
10
11   I don't have any direct interest in the outcome of that suit. I feel it's my duty to provide any
12   information that is relevant to the lawsuit.
13
14   In December YR-3, the Attorney General of Nita, Elizabeth Walters, ordered me to conduct an
15   audit of the Darrow County Circuit Court. We run a routine statistical analysis of all our courts
16   every five years, and irregularities in that analysis prompted the investigation. The analysis
17   showed that Judge Dixon's court was estimated to submit about $500,000 to the state since
18   YR-6, but had submitted only $390,000. I was to perform an audit to determine whether
19   the court was current in submitting the fines and fees it had collected. My audit disclosed a
20   shortfall of approximately $100,000 over more than three years; that the shortfall had been
21   remedied by Court Clerk Sarah Lawton's one-time transfer of $100,000 shortly before I began
22   my audit. Based on this correction, the audit was marked complete.
23
24   As a follow-up, I conducted another audit in August YR-2. That audit revealed another
25     $100,000 of untransferred fines and fees.
26
27   On September 17, YR-2, I notified Judge Dixon of my findings. He replied in a letter dated
28   September 25, YR-2, that he would look into the matter and get back to me, but I didn't hear
29   from him.
30
31   I then spoke to the Attorney General, and she suggested that I request a face-to-face meeting
32   with Judge Dixon. I emailed him requesting a meeting, but he did not respond. I then called
33   him, and he agreed to meet with me at a restaurant in Nita City at 12:00 on November 12. He
34   specifically asked that we not meet at the courthouse.
35
36   On November 12, YR-2, I arrived at the restaurant (Ray's Steakhouse) shortly before noon and
37   waited for the judge for over an hour. At about 1:15, I called his chambers and learned that
38   Judge Dixon had died of gunshot wounds the day before. I had been out of the state, and I
39   didn't know he had died.
40
41   I did not know Judge Dixon personally.

I have read the foregoing transcript of my deposition on the date above and find it is a true and accurate representation of my testimony.

Signed this 30th day of October, YR-1 in Capitol City, Nita

Carter J. Berman

Carter J. Berman

DEPOSITION OF SARAH LAWTON
OCTOBER 18, YR-1, AT SEGAN PRISON FOR WOMEN

1   My name is Sarah Lawton. I reside at the Dianne Segan Prison for Women in Jackson, Nita. I'm
2   fifty-five years old. I'm a widow; my husband died eight years ago. We had one child, Tracy. Tracy
3   died on Christmas Eve, YR-2. It was a heroin overdose. The police thought it was accidental.
4
5   In April YR-1, I was convicted of embezzlement over $10,000 and sentenced to two years. Yes
6   that's a felony. Yes, I pled guilty. Yes, it involved taking money, over the years about $200,000,
7   from the fines and fees that we collected at court.
8
9   I needed the money because Tracy was being threatened by some very bad people. I'm not
10 sure of the details, but it had to do with drugs, opioids. Tracy was a user, on and off, since high
11 school when he got hooked on pain killers after he was injured playing basketball. Eventually
12 he graduated, if that's the right word, from pain killers to heroin. I don't really know whether
13 he sold drugs, but I often thought he did.
14
15 In YR-3, the Nita Attorney General's office started looking into my failure to send in all the
16 fines and fees we had collected. I had then been working for John for about 10 years. I told
17 him the whole story and said that I'd take the consequences even if it meant going to jail.
18 John wouldn't hear of it, and he gave me almost $100,000, which is what the state said was
19 our shortfall. No, it wasn't a loan, it was a gift. John's only condition was that I get Tracy into
20 a substance abuse program, which I did.
21
22 Tracy seemed better for a while but he started with the drugs again, and he came to me for
23 money again. He seemed really scared but he didn't give me any real explanation. And again I
24 took money, another $100,000 from the fines and fees, and gave it to Tracy. By the middle of
25 YR-2 the AG's office was snooping and they wrote to John. He confronted me and I confessed
26 to him. He said he'd try to find another $100,000 but wasn't sure if he could raise it. And
27 believe me; he wasn't happy about the situation. It turned out that he couldn't raise the
28 money and he let me know the day before he died. Yes, by the email that's marked as Exhibit
29 31. That was the last time I heard from John.
30
31 No, I never had a romantic relationship with John. I loved him as a friend, but only as a friend.
32 He was absolutely devoted to Mary. Yes, I once had dinner with John in Capitol City during the
33 State Bar convention. I drove there to talk to him about Tracy. I drove back to Nita City that
34 night. Yes, it's two hours each way.

I absolutely do not believe that John committed suicide. He was 100 percent pro-life and the
most emotionally stable person I ever knew.

Sarah Lawton

Sarah Lawton
October 18, YR-1

ALLISTER E. UPCHURCH, MD

6666 ROTUNDA DR.
WESTCHESTER, NEW YORK
PRACTICE LIMITED TO PSYCHIATRY

November 13, YR-1

Thomas Terwilligen
Barrett & Shaffer
Nita Bank Building
Nita City, Nita 99990

Re: Dixon v. Providential Life Insurance

Dear Mr. Terwilligen:

At your request I have reviewed material you forwarded and have arrived at a conclusion regarding the death of Judge John Dixon. In particular, I have reviewed the following:

1.   Autopsy report

2.   Deposition of Sheriff Khouri

3.   Deposition of Dr. Celli

4.   Deposition of Mary Dixon

5.   Deposition of Robert Wilson

6.   Deposition of Anna Martin

7.   Deposition of Morgan Crowe

8.   Deposition of Carter Berman

9.   Deposition of Sarah Lawton

10.   Correspondence between Mr. Berman and Judge Dixon

11.   Exhibits 1–36

Based on my review of these materials and on my training and experience in psychiatry, it is my opinion that Judge Dixon committed suicide on November 11, YR-2. I base my opinion on the physical evidence that demonstrates that Judge Dixon could easily have pushed the shotgun's trigger with his screwdriver while aiming the gun at his head. The likelihood that an experienced hunter might accidentally discharge a shotgun while aiming it into his left eye is quite remote. I myself am a hunter, and I cannot imagine any shotgun maintenance maneuver that would require positioning a shotgun in that manner.

I also base my opinion of suicide on Judge Dixon's rather well-defined personality and the problems he was facing in the fall of YR-2. Everyone agrees that Judge Dixon was a model of probity. He was one of the community's leading citizens. Obviously, his reputation was very important to him. He faced possible exposure as an unfaithful spouse and as someone who may have abetted embezzlement from his court, and this must have weighed heavily on him. By all accounts, it manifested itself in uncharacteristic behavior including moodiness, desperation, and secretiveness.

We know that Judge Dixon had a desperate need for money, likely for the benefit of Sarah Lawton, his court clerk, to reimburse the state. We know that he pulled many strings to try to obtain that money, but failed. By all accounts, he was not a man accustomed to failure and lacked the psychic reserve to cope with the situation. Moreover, we know that Judge Dixon had already withdrawn money from his accounts without telling his wife. This occurred shortly before Ms. Lawton made a repayment to the state. Now, he was seeking more money at the very time the state was again pressing Ms. Lawton for more repayment. As a forensic psychiatrist, I believe that this is very suspicious for aiding and abetting a felony.

Had this become public, or had a romantic relationship with Ms. Lawton become public, Judge Dixon would have faced the destruction of his spotless personal and professional reputation. This would have been emotionally devastating to this extremely proud man. He could not share his fears and concerns with those closest to him, his family and friends. He kept it all to himself, and of course that only made things worse. He obviously saw suicide as his only way out.

The fact that Judge Dixon shot himself when no one was home is also evidence of suicide. It is quite common for people contemplating suicides to wait for a window of opportunity to take their lives. This eliminates the possibility of a last-minute rescue.

The fact that Judge Dixon left no note for his family is also typical of suicide in a case like this. Judge Dixon killed himself because he was ashamed of what he had made of his life. He certainly was not going to memorialize the circumstances by explaining them in a note. Indeed, he may well have intended to make his death look like an accident. That possibility is supported by his having told so many people about his shotgun problems as well as the fact that he told a number of people that he intended to go hunting that day.

The facts that Judge Dixon seemed to be in a good mood at dinner the night before and that he slept well are also consistent with suicide. We frequently see cases where once someone decides to kill himself, he takes on an air of calm acceptance. It is evidence that a very troubled person has finally found a solution to his problems.

Finally, I should note that Judge Dixon demonstrated several significant risk factors for suicide. He expressed feelings of hopelessness, he faced possible shame if his relationship with Ms. Lawton had been revealed, he had a family history of suicide, and he had access to firearms. Moreover, he was a white male, the demographic group most vulnerable to suicide. The so-called protective factors of family, community, and church support might well have evaporated had the whole picture been made public.

I see nothing in this case that points in any direction other than suicide. Certainly Sheriff Khouri and Dr. Celli are well meaning in reaching their opinions, but they are ill informed about suicide and are obviously influenced by their long friendship with Judge Dixon. No one likes to admit that he did not recognize that a close friend was terribly troubled. It is much easier—and emotionally healthy— to believe that the friend died by accident. The same holds true for Mrs. Dixon and her sister. And certainly for Sarah Lawton.

I will be pleased to testify for you in this case. My charges for review of materials and consultation are $850 per hour, and for testimony, $1,000 per hour.

Very truly yours,

Allister Upchurch

Allister E. Upchurch, MD

ALLISTER E. UPCHURCH, MD
CURRICULUM VITAE

DEGREES:
BA, Columbia College, New York City, YR-28
MD, New York University Medical School, YR-24

POSTGRADUATE TRAINING:
Medical Internship: Boston University Hospital
Psychiatric Residency: Boston University Hospital

ACADEMIC APPOINTMENTS:
Clinical Associate Professor of Psychiatry: New York University Medical School

HOSPITAL PRIVILEGES (In Psychiatry):
Westchester General Hospital
Belleview Hospital

LICENSES:
New York, Massachusetts

CERTIFICATION:
Certified in Psychiatry by American Board of Neurology and Psychiatry, YR-18

PROFESSIONAL MEMBERSHIP:
New York State Medical Society
American Medical Association
Westchester County Medical Society
American Psychiatric Association
New York Psychiatric Association
American Association of Forensic Psychiatrists

PRACTICE:
General inpatient and outpatient psychiatry with special interest in forensic psychiatry.

PUBLICATIONS:
The Role of Junk Food in the Depressive Cascade (YR-20)
Is Rudeness Contagious? (YR-15)
Grief Counseling After the Death of an Abusive Spouse (YR-12)
The Therapeutic Role of Whining (YR-8)
Olfactory Hallucination as a Sign of Psychiatric Illness (YR-5)
Psychotherapy by Email: Has Its Time Come? (YR-4)
Suicide Signs: On the Lookout (YR-3)
"I'm Announcing My Candidacy for President of the United States": An Admission of Psychosis? (YR-2)

JURY INSTRUCTIONS

1. The court will now instruct you on the claims and defenses of the parties and the law governing the case. You must arrive at your verdict by applying the law, as you are now instructed, to the facts as you find them.

   The parties to this case are Mary Dixon, the plaintiff, and Providential Life Insurance Company, the defendant.

   The parties have agreed on, and you must regard as conclusively proven, the following:

   a. The defendant issued a life insurance policy to John Dixon on November 2, YR-2, and the premium of $1,219 was paid.

   b. The insured, John Dixon, died of gunshot wounds on November 11, YR-2, and the life insurance policy was in effect on that date.

   c. The plaintiff is the beneficiary of the life insurance policy.

   d. The face value of the policy is $1 million with a double indemnity clause for accidental death.

   e. The policy has a suicide clause providing that if within two years from the date of the policy the insured shall die by his own hand or act, the liability of the company shall not exceed the amount of the premiums paid.

   f. The plaintiff claims that John Dixon's death was accidental and that she is entitled to recover $2 million under the terms of the life insurance policy—$1 million for the face amount of the policy and $1 million double indemnity for accidental death.

   g. The defendant claims that John Dixon's death was suicide and that under the terms of the life insurance policy, defendant's liability is limited to the amount of the premiums paid of $1,219.

2. The plaintiff has the burden of proving that the insured, John Dixon, died while the life insurance policy was in effect. The parties have agreed, and you must regard as conclusively proven, that John Dixon, the insured, died while the policy was in effect. The plaintiff has the burden of proving her claim that John Dixon's death was accidental. The defendant has the burden of proving its claim that John Dixon's death was a suicide.

3. You are instructed that the life insurance policy issued to the insured, John Dixon, is a contract and that the parties in this case are bound by terms of the contract.

   The life insurance contract has three provisions that are applicable to this case:

   a. The face value of the policy for $1 million payable on proof of death of the insured.

   b. The suicide clause limiting payment to the amount of the premiums paid on proof of suicide by the insured.

   c. The double indemnity accidental clause providing an additional $1 million on proof of accidental death. Under our law, murder is considered "accidental" for purposes of this clause.

4. If you are convinced that the plaintiff has proven by a preponderance of the evidence that the death of the insured, John Dixon, was an accident, then you must return a verdict for the plaintiff in the amount of $2 million.

5. If you are convinced that the defendant has proven by a preponderance of the evidence that the insured, John Dixon, committed suicide, then you must return a verdict for the plaintiff in the amount of the premiums paid, $1,219.

6. In determining whether the death of John Dixon was an accident or a suicide, you are to consider whether his death occurred with his intent or choice. If his death occurred without his intent or choice, then it was an accidental death; if it occurred with his intent or choice, then it was suicide.

7. If you find that the shooting of John Dixon was a homicide, then his death occurred without his intent or choice and against his will, and plaintiff is entitled to recover under the accidental death double indemnity clause of the policy for the full amount of $2 million.

8. You may, but are not required to, infer that John Dixon did not commit suicide because of a human being's natural love of life and hesitancy to die. You are to make your decision from all the facts and evidence in this case.

NITA GENERAL JURY INSTRUCTIONS

Nita Instruction 1:01 Introduction

Members of the jury, the evidence and arguments in this case have been completed, and I will now instruct you as to the law.

The law applicable to this case is stated in these instructions, and it is your duty to follow all of the instructions. You must not single out certain instructions and disregard others.

It is your duty to determine the facts, and to determine them only from the evidence in this case. You are to apply the law to the facts and in this way decide the case. You must not be governed or influenced by sympathy or prejudice for or against any party in this case. Your verdict must be based on evidence and not on speculation, guess, or conjecture.

From time to time, the court has ruled on the admissibility of evidence. You must not concern yourselves with the reasons for these rulings. You should disregard questions and exhibits that were withdrawn or to which objections were sustained.

You should also disregard testimony and exhibits that the court has refused or stricken.

The evidence that you should consider consists only of the witnesses' testimonies and the exhibits the court has received.

Any evidence that was received for a limited purpose should not be considered by you for any other purpose.

You should consider all the evidence in the light of your own observations and experiences in life.

Neither by these instructions nor by any ruling or remark that I have made do I mean to indicate any opinion as to the facts or as to what your verdict should be.

Nita Instruction 1:02 Opening Statements and Closing Arguments

Opening statements are made by the attorneys to acquaint you with the facts they expect to prove. Closing arguments are made by the attorneys to discuss the facts and circumstances in the case and should be confined to the evidence and to reasonable inferences to be drawn therefrom. Neither opening statements nor closing arguments are evidence, and any statement or argument made by the attorneys that is not based on the evidence should be disregarded.

Nita Instruction 1:03 Credibility of Witnesses

You are the sole judges of the credibility of the witnesses and of the weight to be given to the testimony of each witness. In determining what credit is to be given any witness, you may take into account his or her ability and opportunity to observe; his or her manner and appearance while testifying; any interest, bias, or prejudice he or she may have; the reasonableness of the testimony considered in the light of all the evidence; and any other factors that bear on the believability and weight of the witness's testimony.

Nita Instruction 1:04 Expert Witnesses

You have heard evidence in this case from witnesses who testified as experts. The law allows experts to express an opinion on subjects involving their special knowledge, training and skill, experience, or research. While their opinions are allowed to be given, it is entirely within the province of the jury to determine what weight shall be given to their testimony. Jurors are not bound by the testimony of experts; their testimony is to be weighed as that of any other witness.

Nita Instruction 1:05 Direct and Circumstantial Evidence

The law recognizes two kinds of evidence: direct and circumstantial. Direct evidence proves a fact directly—that is, the evidence by itself, if true, establishes the fact. Circumstantial evidence is the proof of facts or circumstances that give rise to a reasonable inference of other facts—that is, circumstantial evidence proves a fact indirectly in that it follows from other facts or circumstances according to common experience and observations in life. An eyewitness is a common example of direct evidence, while human footprints are circumstantial evidence that a person was present.

The law makes no distinction between direct and circumstantial evidence as to the degree or amount of proof required, and each should be considered according to whatever weight or value it may have. All of the evidence should be considered and evaluated by you in arriving at your verdict.

Nita Instruction 1:06 Concluding Instruction

The court did not in any way and does not by these instructions give or intimate any opinions as to what has or has not been proven in the case, or as to what are or are not the facts of the case.

No one of these instructions states all of the law applicable, but all of them must be taken, read, and considered together as they are connected with and related to each other as a whole.

You must not be concerned with the wisdom of any rule of law. Regardless of any opinions you may have as to what the law ought to be, it would be a violation of your sworn duty to base a verdict on any other view of the law than that given in the instructions of the court.

Nita Instruction 2:01 Burden of Proof

When I say that a party has the burden of proof on any issue, or use the expression "if you find," "if you decide," or "by a preponderance of the evidence," I mean that you must be persuaded from a consideration of all the evidence in the case that the issue in question is more probably true than not true.

Any findings of fact you make must be based on probabilities, not possibilities. It may not be based on surmise, speculation, or conjecture.

Nita Instruction 2:02 Corporate Party

One of the parties in this case is a corporation, and it is entitled to the same fair treatment as an individual would be entitled to under like circumstances, and you should decide the case with the same impartiality you would use in deciding a case between individuals.

IN THE CIRCUIT COURT OF
DARROW COUNTY, NITA
CIVIL DIVISION

MARY L. DIXON,	)	
	)	
Plaintiff,	)	
	)	
vs.	)	JURY VERDICT
	)	
PROVIDENTIAL LIFE	)	
INSURANCE COMPANY,	)	
	)	
Defendant.	)	

We, the Jury, return the following verdict, and each of us concurs in this verdict: [Choose **one** of the two following verdicts]

I.

We, the Jury, find that the insured, John Dixon, committed suicide, and the plaintiff is entitled to the amount of the premiums paid, $1,219.

_____
Foreperson

or

II.

We, the Jury, find that the death of the insured, John Dixon, was an accident, and the plaintiff is entitled to the sum of $2,000,000.

_____
Foreperson

EXHIBITS

Exhibit 1

PROVIDENTIAL LIFE INSURANCE COMPANY

Nita Bank Building
Nita City, Nita 99990

Date: October 19, YR-2   Prepared by Robert L. Wilson

LIFE INSURANCE PROFILE FOR JUDGE JOHN J. DIXON

		Disability Waiver of Premiums Accidental Death Benefits	
		$100,000	$1,000,000
1.	**50 years of age* nonsmoker**		
(a)	Yearly Renewable Term	619.00	1,219.00
(b)	Five (5) Year Term	865.60	1,511.00
(c)	Whole Life	3,000.50	4,991.00
2.	**55 years of age* nonsmoker**		
(a)	Yearly Renewable Term	993.50	1,867.00
(b)	Five (5) Year Term	1,515.00	2,510.00
(c)	Whole Life	2,973.00	5,436.00
3.	**60 years of age* nonsmoker**		
(a)	Yearly Renewable Term	1,808.00	2,806.50
(b)	Five (5) Year Term	2,174.50	3,549.00
(c)	Whole Life	3,949.00	6,888.00

Both the yearly renewable term and five-year term are renewable policies, and they are also convertible to Whole Life Insurance on the anniversary date each year. Thus, for the yearly renewable term policy, the insured can renew it each and every year by paying the premium; he need not have a physical examination or do anything else. The same is true for the five-year term policy on the anniversary of the five-year period. The difference between the two term policies is that for the yearly renewable term policy, the premium goes up every year, and for the five-year policy, the premium remains level for the five-year period.

Please Note: This age rate is applicable only until the six (6) month anniversary of the last birthday—November 12, YR-2. After that date, the rate for 51 years of age will be applicable.

Exhibit 2

PROVIDENTIAL LIFE INSURANCE COMPANY

Nita Bank Building
Nita City, Nita 99990

APPLICATION FOR LIFE INSURANCE

Name: John J. Dixon

Address: 5000 Ridge Road, Darrow County, Nita City, Nita

Occupation: Lawyer, Judge

> If less than ten years, please state any other occupations, and the dates thereof, for the ten-year period immediately prior to this application. _____
> If you are presently insured by this or any other company, please list the policies, stating the name of the company, the amount of the insurance, and the date of each policy:
>
> 1. New York Life & Casualty, Co., $50,000 double indemnity, YR-25
> 2. Globe Insurance Co., $30,000 double indemnity, YR-11

Has any coverage ever declined to grant you insurance? (If answer is Yes, state the reasons for the denial of coverage.) No

Date and Place of Birth: Darrow County, Nita, May 12, YR-50

Age at Nearest Birthday: 50

Amount of Insurance Applied For: $1,000,000 & $1,000,000 accidental death

Beneficiary of Policy (To whom the proceeds of the insurance policy should be paid on the death of the applicant):
 Mary L. Dixon

Relationship of Beneficiary to Applicant: Wife

I, John J. Dixon, the applicant herein, hereby represent that the answers and statements made above are true and complete, and agree that they become a part of the contract of insurance if a policy is issued by the Providential Life Insurance Company.

Signature _____*John Dixon*_____ Date 10-26-YR-2

Declaration of Applicant John J. Dixon   Made to Calvin R. Martin, MD

Medical Examiner for the Providential Life Insurance Company, in continuation of and forming a part of the application for insurance.

1. What quantity of malt liquors do you drink daily, if any? Occasional

    Wines? Occasional   Spirits? Occasional

    If not daily, what average? Occasional

2. Have you ever been advised to seek another climate for reasons of health? If so, state details.

    No

3. Have you had a serious illness in the last five years? If so, state details.

    No

4. Have you ever had a surgical operation? If so, state details.

    No

5. Have you ever had albumin, sugar, or blood in urine, or had abnormal blood pressure? If so, state details.

    No

6. Has your weight changed in the last five years? If so, state details.

    No

7. Have you ever used Insulin?

    No

8. Have you consulted, or been attended to by a physician in the last three years? If so, state details.

    Only for minor illnesses — flu, colds, etc. Annual physical

9. Have you ever had any of the following: (Underscore here and give details in space at the end of the declaration): Asthma, Dizziness, Epilepsy, Insanity, Loss of Consciousness, Paralysis, Neuralgia, Frequent or Severe Headaches, Dyspepsia, Gastric or Duodenal Ulcers, Gallstones, Colic, Appendicitis, Chronic Diarrhea, Diseases of Anus or Rectum, Fistula, Rheumatism, Gout, Rupture, Cancer, Tumor, Disease of Kidneys, Bladder, Prostate, Palpitation of Heart, Shortness of Breath, Pain in Chest, Heart Disease, Goiter, Ulcer on any part of body, Stricture, Syphilis, Gonorrhea, AIDS?

    No

10. Do you now live with, or have you lived with or been in close association with, during the past year, any person who has been seriously ill?

    No

11. Has any member of your family committed suicide or attempted to commit suicide? If so, state full details.

    Yes, Mother's brother committed suicide while serving in the Armed Forces

12. Please complete the following family record:

	Age, if living	Age at Death	Date	Cause
Father		84	12/1/YR-14	Age/heart
Mother		84	12/10/YR-13	Age/heart
Brothers	56			
Sisters	48			

I,   John J. Dixon   , an applicant for a life insurance policy from the Providential Life Insurance Company, hereby represents that the above answers and statements made in this Declaration to the Examining Physician for the Company are true and that such answers and statements become part of the contract of insurance if a policy is issued by the Providential Life Insurance Company.

_____   _____
Examining Physician for the Company   Signature of Applicant

  October 26, YR-2   10-26-YR-2
Date   Date

Exhibit 3

PROVIDENTIAL LIFE INSURANCE COMPANY

Nita Bank Building
Nita City, Nita 99990

LIFE INSURANCE POLICY   **POLICY NO. 712089**

THE PROVIDENTIAL LIFE INSURANCE COMPANY, hereinafter referred to as THE COMPANY, IN CONSIDERATION of the Application for this Policy, said Application being hereby made a part of this Contract, and a copy of same being attached hereto, and in further consideration of the payment of premiums hereinafter stated, hereby insured the life of

JOHN J. DIXON,

hereinafter referred to as THE INSURED.

1. FACE AMOUNT OF POLICY — $1,000,000, payable at THE COMPANY'S Home Office, Nita Bank Building, Nita City, Nita, upon legal surrender of this Policy at said Office, and upon due proof of death of THE INSURED, to

MARY L. DIXON,

   beneficiary and wife of THE INSURED, or if said beneficiary is not living at the date of death of her husband, said INSURED, to the Executor or Administrator of THE INSURED.

2. BENEFIT IN EVENT OF DEATH BY ACCIDENT — $1,000,000, payable at Home Office of THE COMPANY, said benefit being in addition to the FACE AMOUNT herein, subject to the provisions hereinafter set forth.

3. ANNUAL PREMIUM — $1,219, payable to THE COMPANY on delivery of the Policy, and a like amount is due on the 1st day of November one year thereafter and in each succeeding year. Said premium includes an extra annual premium of $100 for the Benefit payable in Event of Death by Accident.

4. SUICIDE OF INSURED — If, within two years from the date of delivery of this Policy, THE INSURED shall die by his own hand or act, the liability of THE COMPANY shall not exceed the amount of the premiums theretofore paid on this Policy.

5. INCONTESTABILITY — This Policy shall be incontestable after two years from the date of delivery hereof except for nonpayment of premiums.

6. STATEMENTS IN APPLICATION — All Statements made by THE INSURED in applying for this Policy and all statements made by him in the course of medical examination by THE COMPANY'S physicians or medical examiners upon application for this Policy shall be deemed representations and not warranties.

7. BENEFIT IN EVENT OF ACCIDENTAL DEATH is payable upon due proof by the beneficiary that the death of THE INSURED occurred as a result, directly or indirectly and independent of all other causes, of bodily injuries effected solely through external, violent, and accidental means, of which, except in the case of drowning or of internal injuries revealed by an autopsy, there is a visible contusion or wound on the exterior of the body, and that such death occurred within 90 days of the accident and during the continuance of this Policy while there was no default in payment of any premiums.

8. THE INSURED reserves the right to change the beneficiary herein upon due notice to THE COMPANY.

IN WITNESS WHEREOF, THE PROVIDENTIAL LIFE INSURANCE COMPANY has caused this Policy to be executed and duly attested at its Home Office in Nita City, Nita, on the 2nd day of November, YR-2, which is the date of issue and delivery of this Policy to THE INSURED.

SECRETARY   PRESIDENT

Issuing Age: 50

Exhibit 4

Robert Wilson

From: Robert Wilson
Sent: January 22, YR-1
To: Mary Dixon <librarymary22@mail.nita>
Subject: Life Insurance Policy No. 712089
Attachments: Ltr-712089.doc

Dear Mrs. Dixon:

Please find attached a letter from Providential Life Insurance regarding your insurance claim. If you have any questions, please do not hesitate to call me.

Robert L. Wilson
General Manager
Providential Life Insurance Company
Nita Bank Building
Nita City, Nita 99990
M: 819.555.2277
Email: rwilson@provlife.nita

PROVIDENTIAL LIFE INSURANCE COMPANY

Nita Bank Building
Nita City, Nita 99990

January 22, YR-1

Mrs. Mary Dixon
5000 Ridge Road
Nita City, Nita 99995

Re: John J. Dixon
         Policy No. 712089

Dear Mrs. Dixon:

We acknowledge receipt of your claim for accidental death benefits on the above-numbered Life Insurance Policy, a copy of the death certificate for John J. Dixon, and the above-numbered policy issued to John J. Dixon.

We have carefully considered your claim for accidental death benefits of $2 million under paragraph 2 of the policy. The Company regrets to inform you that it must deny any liability to you under the terms of the policy other than to remit the amount of premiums paid by the insured, John J. Dixon, in the sum of $1,219. A check in that amount will be enclosed with the hard copy of this letter.

The Company acknowledges that said Policy was issued to your late husband, John J. Dixon, and that you are the beneficiary under said Policy. The Company also acknowledges that the insured, John J. Dixon, died at his residence on November 11, YR-2, as the result of a wound or wounds sustained in the discharge of his shotgun. We regret to advise you that the Company is compelled to take the position that the death of the insured was not accidental as you claim, but, as the evidence available to the Company indicates, the insured took his own life. Accordingly, since this unfortunate event occurred within two years from the date of the issuance of the Policy, the only liability of the Company under the terms of the Policy is the return of the premiums paid.

The Policy issued by us and duly presented to us by you is returned to you herewith.

The Company regrets the circumstances of the claim and extends to you deepest sympathies. We trust that you will understand the position we are forced to take with regard to it.

Yours very truly,

ss/Robert L. Wilson
Robert L. Wilson
General Manager

RLW:am

Exhibit 5

Providential Life Insurance Company

Nita Bank Building
Nita City, Nita 99990

January 22, YR-1

Mrs. Mary Dixon
5000 Ridge Road
Nita City, Nita 99995

Re: John J. Dixon
        Policy No. 712089

Dear Mrs. Dixon:

We acknowledge receipt of your claim for accidental death benefits on the above-numbered Life Insurance Policy, a copy of the death certificate for John J. Dixon, and the above-numbered policy issued to John J. Dixon.

We have carefully considered your claim for accidental death benefits of $2 million under paragraph 2 of the policy. The Company regrets to inform you that it must deny any liability to you under the terms of the policy other than to remit the amount of premiums paid by the insured, John J. Dixon, in the sum of $1,219. A check in that amount is enclosed.

The Company acknowledges that said Policy was issued to your late husband, John J. Dixon, and that you are the beneficiary under said Policy. The Company also acknowledges that the insured, John J. Dixon, died at his residence on November 11, YR-2, as the result of a wound or wounds sustained in the discharge of his shotgun. We regret to advise you that the Company is compelled to take the position that the death of the insured was not accidental as you claim, but, as the evidence available to the Company indicates, the insured took his own life. Accordingly, since this unfortunate event occurred within two years from the date of the issuance of the Policy, the only liability of the Company under the terms of the Policy is the return of the premiums paid.

The Policy issued by us and duly presented to us by you is returned to you herewith.

The Company regrets the circumstances of the claim and extends to you deepest sympathies. We trust that you will understand the position we are forced to take with regard to it.

Yours very truly,

Robert L. Wilson

Robert L. Wilson
General Manager

RLW:am
Enc.

Exhibit 5A

PROVIDENTIAL LIFE INSURANCE COMPANY   **1093**
Nita Bank Building
Nita City, Nita 99990   <u>January 18</u> YR <u>-1</u> 33-3434/2712

PAY TO THE
ORDER OF   <u>Mary L. Dixon</u> $ <u>1,219.00</u>

<u>One thousand, two hundred and nineteen 00/00</u>   DOLLARS

NITA NATIONAL BANK
Nita City, Nita 99990

Robert L. Wilson
Robert L. Wilson, General Manager

:271274241:   26··838 3·   1093

Exhibit 6

Robert Wilson

From: Mary Dixon <mdixon@nitanet.nita>
Sent: January 25, YR-1
To: Robert Wilson < rwilson@provlife.nita>
Subject: Re: Life Insurance Policy No. 712089

Dear Sir:

I received your letter of January 22 and your check for $1,219. My husband's death was accidental, not a suicide, and I can prove this. You clearly owe me the double indemnity that your policy provides. If you don't honor your policy, I'll have to see a lawyer and sue your company. Meanwhile, I'm not going to cash the check you sent. You should be ashamed of yourself.

Mary Dixon

From: Robert Wilson [mailto: rwilson@provlife.nita]
Sent: January 22, YR-1
To: Mary Dixon
Subject: Life Insurance Policy No. 712089

Dear Mrs. Dixon:

Please find attached a letter from Providential Life Insurance regarding your insurance claim. If you have any questions, please do not hesitate to call me.

Robert L. Wilson
General Manager
Providential Life Insurance Company
Nita Bank Building
Nita City, Nita 99990
M: 819.555.2277
Email: rwilson@provlife.nita

Exhibit 7

**OFFICE OF THE
ATTORNEY GENERAL**

STATE OF NITA

AUDIT & INVESTIGATIONS DIVISION
400 CAPITOL BUILDING
CAPITOL CITY, NITA 99999

September 17, YR-2

Hon. John J. Dixon
5000 Ridge Road
Nita City, Nita 99995

Dear Judge Dixon:

I am taking the liberty of writing to you at home for reasons that will be obvious.

On orders from the Attorney General, I am checking the transfer to the State of fines and fees collected by the Darrow County Circuit Court. I am sure you are familiar with the requirements of Section 102 of the Nita Uniform County Courts Act, which require transfer of all such monies to the State within thirty days of collection.

I have audited your court's records and have found disturbing irregularities. Between YR-6 and YR-3, approximately $100,000 was collected by the court, but not transferred to the State as required. In late YR-3, the full amount was transferred by Sarah Lawton, Darrow County Circuit Court Clerk, without explanation of the timing except for an "apology" for the tardiness. Between that time and this to date, another $100,000 should have been transferred, but was not. I called Ms. Lawton in early August, and she promised to look into the matter and get back to me promptly. I have not heard from her since then, and she has not returned my subsequent calls.

Please look into this matter and let me know what you find. Thank you.

Sincerely,

Carter J. Berman

Carter J. Berman
Auditor & Investigator

CJB:alr

Exhibit 8

John J. Dixon
5000 Ridge Road
Darrow County
Nita City, Nita 99995
(819) 555-3632
jjdix@nita.nita

September 25, YR-2

Carter J. Berman
Office of the Attorney General
400 Capitol Building
Capitol City, Nita 99999

Dear M. Berman:

I have received your letter of September 17.

Please understand that Ms. Lawton is a long-time, trusted employee who has undergone significant emotional distress since her husband's death a few years ago. I am certain her failure to transfer funds is a consequence of nothing more sinister than inadvertence.

I will give this matter my immediate attention and will do my best to close the matter very shortly. Thank you for your anticipated patience and understanding.

Yours truly,

John J. Dixon

Exhibit 9

Carter J. Berman

From: Carter J. Berman
Sent: October 23, YR-2
To: John Dixon <jjdix@nita.nita >
Subject: Letter of September 17, YR-2

Dear Judge Dixon:

Please refer to my letter of September 17, YR-2, and your reply of September 25.

In your letter you promised that you would give the matter your immediate attention, but I have not heard anything more from you. I turn, therefore, to email in an effort to obtain a response.

I would like to meet with you in person, and I suggest the week of November 2. Please advise.

Sincerely,

Carter J. Berman
Auditor & Investigator
State of Nita
Office of the Attorney General
400 Capitol Building
Capitol City, Nita 99999
819.555.4238, ext. 754
cjburns@stateag.nita

Exhibit 10

Diagram of Shotgun

The shotgun found next to Judge Dixon's body is a Browning B-SS28, 12-gauge, single-barrel, single-shot shotgun. It has a lever on the top of the pistol-grip (tang) portion of the stock, which when pushed opens (or "breaks") the barrel at the breach where the shotgun shell is inserted. Just behind the lever on the top of the tang is a safety button, which slides forward to the "on" position and backwards to the "off" position. The "on" position means that the safety is on, and the shotgun will not discharge when the trigger is pulled; the "off" position means that the safety is off, and the shotgun will discharge when the trigger is pulled.

The gun barrel is thirty inches from the end of the muzzle to the breach. It is thirty-two inches from the muzzle end to the single trigger. Overall, from end to end, muzzle to butt, the shotgun is forty-six and three-quarters inches. The barrel has a modified choke (it narrows to keep the shot close together on discharge), and the gun weighs seven pounds.

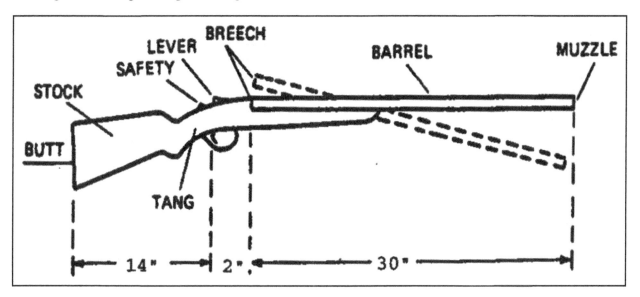

Exhibit 11

Diagram of Skull Prepared by Dr. Celli

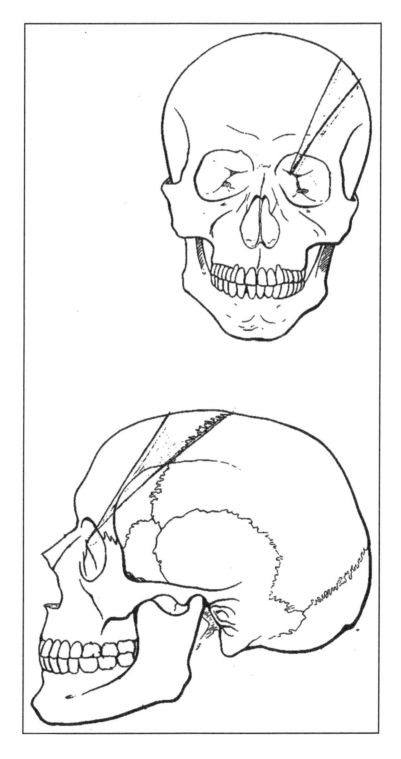

Diagram of Dixon House

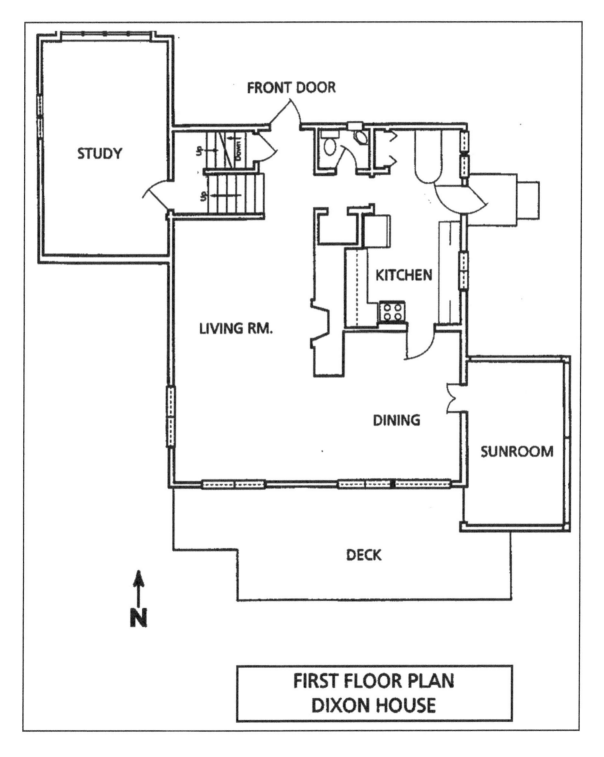

FIRST FLOOR PLAN
DIXON HOUSE

Exhibit 13

Diagram of Dixon Study

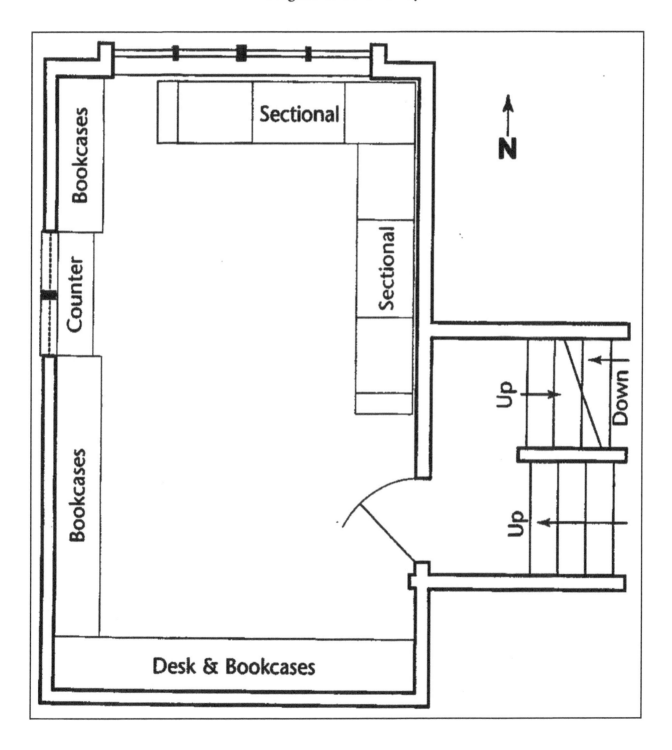

Exhibit 14

Crowe, Morgan F.

From: Robert Wilson [rwilson@provlife.nita]
Sent: November 20, YR-2 1:40 p.m.
To: Morgan Crowe
Subject: John Dixon

Norm –

Good to see you today and to chat with you. Yes, John's death is a terrible tragedy. I'm especially interested in what you had to say about how desperate he seemed to you shortly before he killed himself. I have a feeling that Mary is going to try to profit from all this, and you might be called on to recount your last contacts with John.

On another matter, I'm still working on getting some Providential business to you, and I'm pretty optimistic.

Best,

Bob

Exhibit 15

Crowe, Morgan F.

From: Tom Gross [tgross@pineweaver.nita]
Sent: August 1, YR-2 10:26 a.m.
To: Sales list
Subject: Green By Green

This fund presents substantial upside, short-term potential. As with any alternative-energy offering—however, there is significant risk. It should, therefore, be offered only to clients with a net worth of at least $500,000.

The fund is eager to raise capital and has offered an incentive commission, in addition to the usual 5% cash commission, of 1/10 share of stock for each share we sell. We will pay the incentive commission to the selling broker.

Tom Gross
CEO
Pine Weaver Investments

(Note: This email was obtained by subpoena after Morgan Crowe's deposition.)

Exhibit 16

Photograph of Judge Dixon Taken the Summer before His Death

Exhibit 17

Photographs Taken by Altair Khouri at the Death Scene
(Exhibits 17–25)

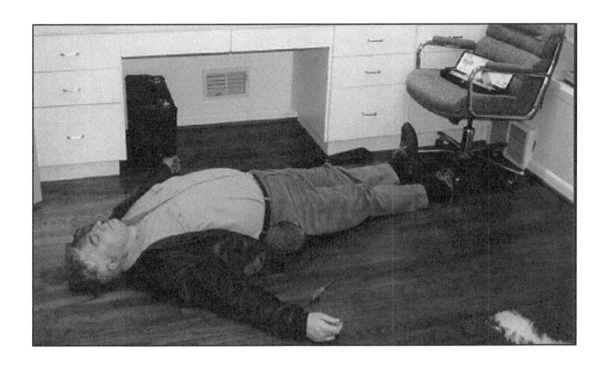

Exhibit 18

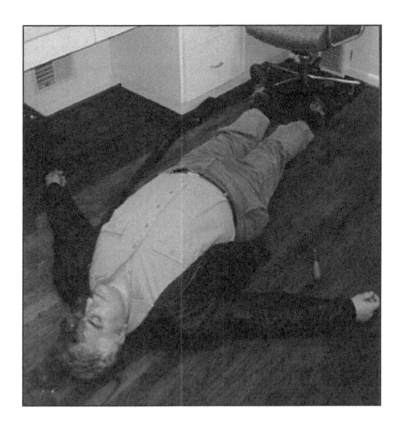

Exhibit 19

Exhibit 20

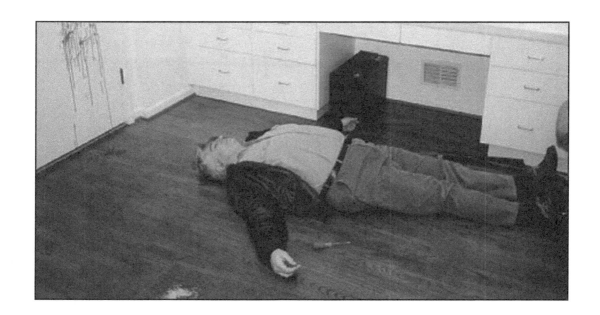

Exhibit 21

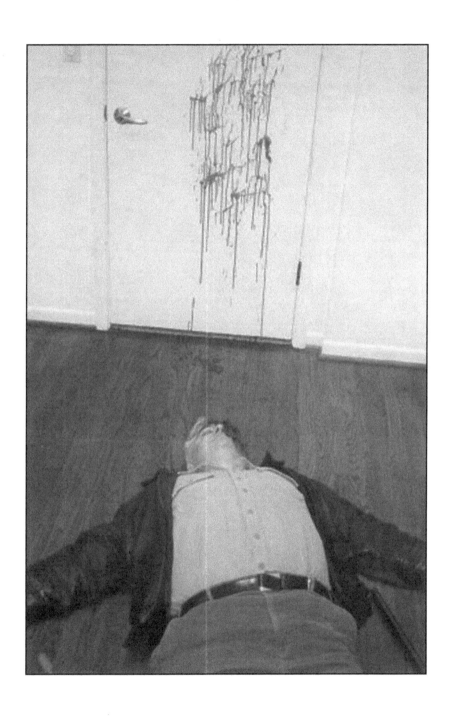

Exhibit 22

Exhibit 23

Exhibit 24

Exhibit 25

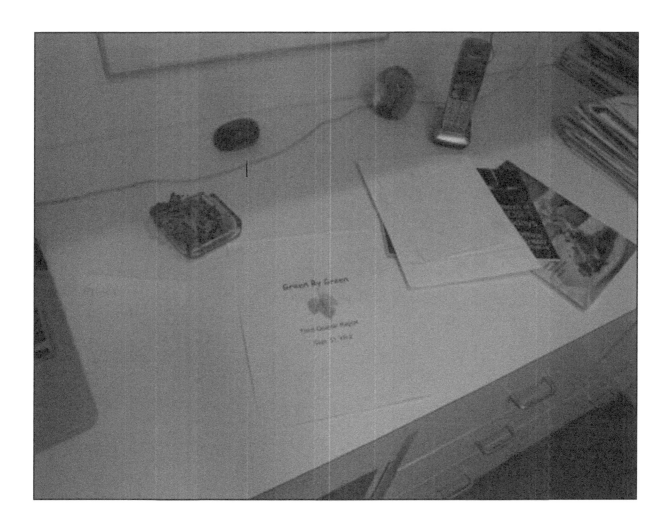

Exhibit 26

Photographs Taken by Altair Khouri
after the Investigation at the Death Scene
(Exhibits 26–29)

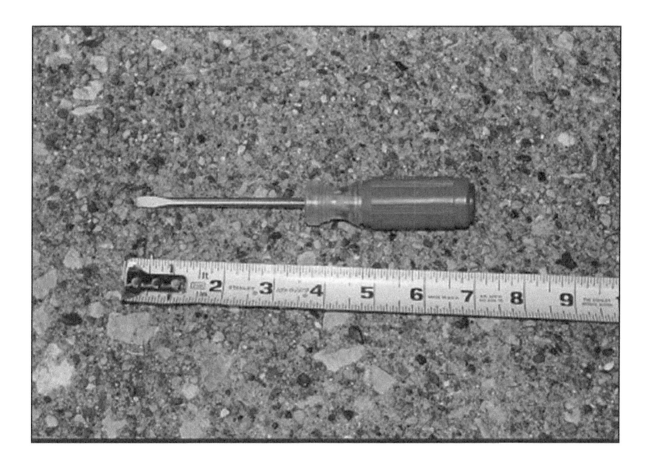

Exhibit 27

Exhibit 28

Exhibit 29

Exhibit 30

Email Chain printed from Judge Dixon's computer
between Judge Dixon and "Tracy"

John Dixon

From: Tracy [tlawt@nita.nita]
Sent: November 9, YR-2 11:40 p.m.
To: John J. Dixon
Subject: Mom

You going to take responsibility for what you've done Mr. Bigshot?

From: John J. Dixon [jjdix@nita.nita]
Sent: November 9, YR-2 11:35 p.m.
To: Tracy
Subject: Mom

Tracy:

Trying my best but not very optimistic. Looks like it's finally time for you to take responsibility for the havoc you've caused.

John

From: Tracy [tlawt@nita.nita]
Sent: November 9, YR-2 11:15 p.m.
To: John J. Dixon
Subject: Mom

Judge D.

Mom is really feeling the heat and beginning to panic. We need to get 100K to her ASAP. I'm afraid that if she can't make a big payment all hell will break loose and she'll spill the beans. That will lead to the last payment she made and that will lead to the source of the money, and that will lead to questions you don't want asked.

Exhibit 31

Email printed from Judge Dixon's computer to "Sarah"

John Dixon

From: John J. Dixon [jjdix@nita.nita]
Sent: November 10, YR-2 8:45 p.m.
To: Sarah
Subject: Status

Dear Sarah:

I'm afraid that, as expected, I can't raise the money and we'll all just have to face the consequences. Tracy has agreed to stop by later tonight and I'll break the news to him. I'm going hunting with Al Khouri tomorrow. I'll explain the situation and seek counsel. Sorry.

John

Exhibit 32

Browser History

Exhibit 33

911 Transcript

Operator: 911, what is your emergency?

Caller: It's my husband, he's dead. He's been shot in the head.

Operator: Has someone shot your husband?

Caller: No, no, he shot himself. It's a horrible accident. Oh, my god.

Operator: Where are you, ma'am?

Caller: At home, 5000 Ridge Road, in Nita City.

Operator: I'm dispatching an ambulance and a sheriff's car right now. Are you certain your husband is dead, ma'am?

Caller: Yes, yes, he's dead. His head is blown away.

Operator: What is your name, ma'am?

Caller: Mary Dixon. My husband is Judge John Dixon.

Operator: Is there anyone else at home with you, Mrs. Dixon?

Caller: No, just John and me.

Operator: Can you contact anyone to come to your house to wait with you for the ambulance and sheriff's car?

Caller: I don't know. Yes, I think my neighbor is home. She'll come over.

Operator: Good. The ambulance and sheriff's car should be there within five minutes. Do you want me to call your neighbor for you?

Caller: No, I can do it.

Operator: OK, do it right now. And please don't touch anything where your husband is. Leave that for the deputies.

Caller: OK, OK. Thank you. [Hangs up.]

(Note: This audio recording is available at http://bit.ly/1P20Jea
Password: Dixon7)

Exhibit 34

Text Chain from Altair Khouri's Cell Phone

Exhibit 35

COUNTY OF DARROW OFFICE OF THE CORONER

CERTIFICATE OF DEATH

STATE OF NITA
USE BLACK INK ONLY

CERTIFICATE NUMBER

000113

NAME OF DECENDENT—LAST	FIRST		MIDDLE	
DIXON	JOHN		J.	

ALSO KNOWN AS	DATE OF BIRTH	AGE	SEX	SOCIAL SECURITY NUMBER
NONE	5/12/YR-50	50	M	999-32-628

STATE/COUNTRY OF BIRTH	EVER SERVED IN U.S. ARMED FORCES?	MARITAL STATUS (at time of death)	DATE OF DEATH (mm/dd/yyyy)	TIME (24 hours)
NITA	Y__ N_X_ UNK__	MARRIED	11/11/YR-2	09:45

EDUCATION	USUAL OCCUPATION	KIND OF BUISNESS OR INDUSTRY	YEARS IN OCCUPATION	WAS DECEDANT HISPANIC/LATINO	DECENDANT'S RACE
JD	JUDGE	LAW	10	NO	CAUCASIAN

DECEDANT'S ADDRESS
5000 RIDGE ROAD

CITY	COUNTY	STATE	YEARS IN COUNTY
NITA CITY	DARROW	NITA	55

IDENTIFICATION INFORMATION

IDENTIFICATION BY:	RELATIONSHIP
(1) ALEX SHARPE, (2) MARY DIXON	(1) CORONER, (2) WIDOW OF DECEASED

SPOUSE AND PARENT INFORMATION

NAME OF SURVIVING SPOUSE—LAST	FIRST	MIDDLE	MAIDEN NAME
DIXON	MARY	L.	MARTIN

NAME OF FATHER—LAST	FIRST	MIDDLE	STATE OF BIRTH
DIXON	HOWARD	W.	NITA

NAME OF MOTHER—MAIDEN	FIRST	MIDDLE	STATE OF BIRTH
BRADFORD	PATRICIA	D.	NITA

PLACE OF DEATH INFORMATION

PLACE OF DEATH	COUNTY	ADDRESS AT LOCATION WHERE FOUND
RESIDENCE	DARROW	5000 RIDGE ROAD, NITA CITY, NITA

CAUSE OF DEATH INFORMATION

CAUSE OF DEATH	WAS THE DEATH CAUSED BY:
GUNSHOT WOUND TO THE HEAD	NATURAL CAUSES __ ACCIDENT _X_ SUICIDE __ HOMICIDE __

WAS AN AUTOPSY PERFORMED?	DATE	LOCATION
YES	11/12/YR-2	DARROW COUNTY MORGUE

MEDICAL EXAMINER'S CONCLUSION OF CAUSE OF DEATH
SELF-INFLICTED, ACCIDENTAL GUNSHOT WOUND TO THE LEFT SIDE OF THE HEAD

SIGNATURE OF MEDICAL EXAMINER	DATE	TYPED/PRINTED NAME OF MEDICAL EXAMINER
Edward E. Sharpe	NOVEMBER 12, YR-2	E. E. SHARPE

CERTIFICATION

I, **Able Ames**, Clerk of the Office of the Coroner of Darrow County, State of Nita, do hereby certify that I am in charge of the records of this office, and that the above Death Certificate is a correct and accurate copy of the original on file in this Office.

Date: **11/12/YR-2**

_____
Clerk, Office of the Coroner

Exhibit 36

Darrow County

Office of the Medical Examiner
Nita City, Nita 99990

AUTOPSY REPORT

DIXON, JOHN J.

DATE AND TIME OF EXAMINATION:	12 November YR-2 at 3:00 p.m.
PLACE OF EXAMINATION:	Darrow County Morgue
	Nita City, Nita
AUTOPSY PERFORMED BY:	E. S. Celli, MD

EXTERNAL EXAMINATION

The body is that of a well-developed and nourished white man whose appearance is consistent with his listed age of fifty years. The length is seventy-two inches and estimated weight is 200 pounds. The body is well preserved and has not been embalmed. Rigidity is fully developed in the jaw and extremities, and lividity is dorsal. The body is cool to the touch.

The face and scalp are the site of the injuries to be described. The scalp is covered with medium-length, gray and gray-brown hair. The external ears are normally formed and located. The right iris is brown, cornea dull, and conjunctivae unremarkable. The left eye is destroyed. The nose is intact, and blood is present in the nares. The lips and tongue are intact, and the teeth are natural and in good condition. Blood is present in the mouth. There is sooting in the area of the wound. Under the sooting, powder is imbedded in the skin.

The neck is symmetrical and trachea in the midline. The chest is symmetrical and normally formed. The abdomen is slightly protuberant and soft. The external genitalia are uncircumcised adult male. The back is straight and symmetrical.

The arms are symmetrical and normally formed. The nail beds are cyanotic. The fingernails are neatly trimmed and clean. On the palm and flexor aspects of the fingers of the left hand there is a small amount of diffuse, black soiling, which may represent gunpowder fouling. The legs are normally formed. No edema is present.

No identifying marks or surgical scars are noted. No needle punctures or tracks are identified.

EVIDENCE OF INJURY

Shotgun Wound

ENTRANCE WOUND: A shotgun entrance wound is present over the left eye and the nasion. This is at the inferio-medial aspect of the lacerated wound to be described below and is at a point four and one-half inches below the top of the head and one inch to the left of the midline. There is a margin of dense fouling and burning, which measures one fourth of an inch in width over the inferior and medial aspects of the wound. An elliptical area of less dense fouling extends from the medial aspect of the left orbit to the left ear and from the zygoma to the left frontal region. Relative to the entrance wound, this measures two inches in width at the twelve o'clock position, four inches at the three o'clock position, one and one-half inches at the six o'clock position, and one-half inch at the nine o'clock position.

PATH OF MISSILES: The missiles passed through the orbit, destroying the eye. They then passed through the orbital roof and continued through the left frontal lobe of the brain, pulpifying it. The missiles also passed along and through the left frontal bone of the skull, which is comminuted.

EXIT WOUND: The bulk of the missiles exited through a gaping, lacerated wound that measures five by two inches and extends from the left orbit to the left frontoparietal region, with its long axis oriented from anterio-inferior to posterio-superior at an angle of approximately forty-five degrees. This wound is in continuity with the entrance wound.

RECOVERY OF MISSILES: Several lead shotgun pellets and a felt wad are recovered in the pulpified brain tissue.

COURSE OF WOUND: Relative to the erect body the missiles passed from front to back, from below upward, and from right to left.

The description of these injuries will not be repeated under the internal examination.

INTERNAL EXAMINATION

BODY CAVITIES: There is no abnormal fluid in the cavities, and the serosal surfaces are smooth and glistening. The mediastinum and retroperitoneum are unremarkable and the leaves of the diaphragm intact. The organs are anatomically disposed.

CARDIOVASCULAR SYSTEM: The heart has its normal shape, and size and the pericardium is smooth and glistening. The coronary arteries arise and are distributed in the usual manner with right dominance, and they show slight atherosclerotic plaques, which do not cause significant stenosis. The endocardium is smooth and glistening, and the cardiac valves are unremarkable. The myocardium is reddish-brown and firm and shows no focal lesions. The aorta follows its usual course, and its intima is the site of slight atherosclerotic plaquing. The origins of the major arteries and great vessels of venous return are unremarkable.

RESPIRATORY SYSTEM: The larynx, trachea, and bronchi contain a small amount of blood. Their mucosa is unremarkable. The lungs have their normal shape, and lobation and the pleura is smooth and glistening. They retain their shape on removal and are slightly firm and subcrepitant to palpitation. The cut surfaces are moist and exude a small amount of bloody, foamy fluid on digital pressure. There is no enlargement or consolidation of the airspaces. The pulmonary arteries are normally disposed and patent.

URINARY SYSTEM: The kidneys have their normal shape and size. Their capsules strip with ease, revealing smooth external surfaces. Cut surfaces show the usual corticomedullary architecture. The pelves and ureters are unremarkable. The bladder is empty. Its mucosa is intact.

INTERNAL GENITALIA: The prostate and testes are unremarkable.

LYMPHORETICULAR SYSTEM: The spleen is of usual size, and its capsule is intact. Cut surfaces show the usual features. The thymus is involuted. The lymph nodes are unremarkable.

GASTROINTESTINAL SYSTEM: The esophagus is unremarkable. The stomach contains an estimated 50 ml of dark brown fluid. Its mucosa is intact and continuous with an unremarkable duodenum. The small and large intestines are unremarkable. The appendix is present.

HEPATOBILIARY SYSTEM: The liver has its usual size and shape. The capsule is intact, and the cut surfaces show the usual lobular architecture. The gall bladder contains approximately 30 ml of bile, and its mucosa is unremarkable. The bile ducts are normally disposed.

ENDOCRINE SYSTEM: The pituitary, thyroid, adrenals, and pancreas are unremarkable.

MUSCULOSKELETAL SYSTEM: No fractures are identified. The bone marrow, where visualized, is unremarkable. The skeletal muscle has its usual color and texture.

NECK ORGANS: There is no hemorrhage in the soft tissues. The cartilaginous and bony structures are intact.

HEAD: The scalp, skull, and brain are the site of the previously described injuries. Where preserved, the leptomeninges are glistening and transparent, and the gyri have their usual configuration. The vessels at the base of the brain are normally disposed and show no atherosclerosis. Except for the shotgun wound, the cut surfaces show no abnormalities. Removal of the dura from the base of the skull shows only the previously described injuries.

PATHOLOGICAL FINDINGS

Shotgun wound to head.

1. Close contact entrance wound in left eye.

2. Pulpifaction of left frontal lobe of brain and comminution of left orbital roof and left frontal bone.

3. Exit wound in left frontal region.

4. Missiles recovered in brain.

5. Course of wound: front to back, below upward, and right to left (see attached diagram).

OPINION

The decedent was found dead in his home. Autopsy showed the cause of death to be a close contact shotgun wound of the head. Based on the nature of the wound, the findings at the scene, and the background history of the decedent, the manner of death is considered accidental.

Emery S. Celli

E. S. Celli, MD

Medical Examiner, Darrow County

IMPEACHMENT PROBLEMS

Problem 1

Assume that Robert Wilson testified on direct exam that he now recalls that he saw the check marks on the policy when Mrs. Dixon gave it to him on November 18. For the plaintiff, impeach Wilson from his deposition.

Problem 2

Assume that when asked on direct examination whether Green By Green paid a commission on the investment by Judge Dixon, Morgan Crowe testified consistently with his deposition that Green By Green paid a standard 5 percent commission on the sale. For the plaintiff, impeach Crowe on failure to disclose the extra commission.

Problem 3

Assume that Sheriff Khouri testified on direct exam that, when Khouri last spoke with John Dixon, Dixon told him that he thought he had discovered the problem with his Browning and had fixed it. For the defendant, impeach Sheriff Khouri from his deposition.

Problem 4

Assume that Mary Dixon testified on direct exam that she is certain there were no check marks on the policy when she gave it to Wilson. For the defendant, impeach Mrs. Dixon from her deposition.